MW01122306

The Last
Journey of
Captain
Harte

The Last Journey of Captain Harte

Dianne Warren

NUAGE
EDITIONS

Acknowledgments
The author wishes to thank:
For financial and/or workshop support—the Canada Council for the Arts; the Saskatchewan Playwrights Centre; Globe Theatre, Regina; Theatre Passe Muraille, Toronto.
For faith in her plays—Tom Bentley-Fisher.
For dramaturgical advice—Marina Endicott, Connie Gault, Banuta Rubess.
For translating dialogue for the first production—Satpal Singh Virdi and Prakasha Kaur Virdi.
The song "Cool Water" referred to in Scene 9 was written by Bob Nolan (words and music). Rights are controlled by Unichappell Music Inc.

Cover design by Doowah Design.
Photograph of Dianne Warren by Don Hall.
Published with the assistance of The Canada Council for the Arts.
Printed and bound in Canada by Veilleux Impression à Demande.

Canadian Cataloguing in Publication Data

       Warren, Dianne, date
           The last journey of Captain Harte

       (Performance Series)
       A play.
       ISBN 0-921833-63-6

              I. Title.   II. Series: Performance series (Winnipeg ,Man.)

PS8595.A778L38 1999   C812'.54   C99900282-1
PR9199.3.W366L38 1999

Nuage Editions, P.O. Box 206, RPO Corydon
Winnipeg, MB, R3M 3S7

In memory of my father,
Calvin Ray Warren

Production History

The Last Journey of Captain Harte was first performed by Twenty-fifth Street Theatre in Saskatoon, Saskatchewan, directed by Tom Bentley-Fisher. It opened on January 31, 1997 with the following cast:

Marguerite:	Valerie Ann Pearson
Ruben:	Jim Leyden
Joel:	Christopher Lee Fassbender
Harte:	Joe Welsh
Mr. Sealey:	David Edney
Nurse #1/Various characters:	Satpal Singh Virdi
Beauty/Nurse #2:	Anne Simmie

Set & Lighting Design:	Colin Ross
Costumes:	Penny Paget
Stage Manager:	Angus Ferguson

Characters

Marguerite:
> A woman, fiftyish, who lives on a farm just outside the fictitious town of St. James in south-western Saskatchewan.

Harte:
> A nomadic friend of Marguerite's long-dead husband.

Ruben:
> Marguerite's older brother, who suffers from a degenerative disease, characterized by muscle weakness and fatigue.

Joel:
> Marguerite's seventeen-year-old son.

Mr. Sealey:
> Seventy years old or so. A gardener.

Beauty:
> Ruben's wife.

Various people in Asia, all played by the same male actor:
> A nurse, a hotel operator, a flower seller, a black market businessman. The language(s) spoken by these characters could vary, depending upon language(s) spoken by the actor cast. In the first production, the characters spoke Hindi and Urdu.

A second nurse at the end of the play:
> Played by the same actor who plays Beauty.

Time and Place
> Most of the play is set on Marguerite's farm. Several scenes take place in non-specific locations in Asia. The time is the present.

A Note to the Reader
> The Asian scenes in the play have characters that speak languages such as Hindi, Urdu or Thai. In this text, their speeches are presented in English and are indicated by square brackets. It is important to note that on stage they are to be subtitled or surtitled in English, with the result that the audience understands what's going on, but Captain Harte doesn't.

ACT I

Scene 1

Mr. Sealey, arms full of gardening tools, is looking at Marguerite's garden. Marguerite is in a lawn chair, letter in hand. They're in two different spaces.

Mr. Sealey: *(Studying the garden.)* I don't like the looks of this, not one bit. Very odd. Very unusual.

Marguerite: He's sorry, he says. Sorry about Andrew. My dear brother.

Mr. Sealey: Well. Something is not right, that's for certain. I could suggest the library. Or perhaps the research station. But one doesn't like to presume.

Joel: *(Voice from off stage.)* Mom? What's for supper tonight?

Marguerite: Ruben's coming. What's for supper tonight? I should just call up the travel agency and book myself onto that cruise old Mrs. Rorke goes on every year. January would be the more appropriate month, but why not June or July? Why not? A cruise, yes. Fancy meals, dinner with the captain. And I mustn't forget the waiters, handsome young men. There's one named Raoul, who blew ever so gently in Mrs. Rorke's ear at every meal and turned her into a young woman again, for a few seconds at least. A waiter who blows in your ear. Such service. Such kindness.

Joel: *(From off stage.)* Mom? I'm picking Stevie up at seven, so I want to eat early. Mom?

Marguerite: He says he's coming to help me out. That's a good one.

Mr. Sealey: Every man his own gardener. Or every woman as the case may be. So much to do. So much to accomplish.

Mr. Sealey exits.

Scene 2

Harte is in a hospital bed somewhere in Thailand. He has a thermometer in his mouth. A nurse enters and reads the thermometer. The nurse speaks English.

Nurse: You're doing better, Mr. Harte.

Harte: Back from the dead.

Nurse: Temperature's down. No chills. No fever.

Harte: Thank God for wonder drugs, eh?

Nurse: Oh, I don't know about wonder drugs. And there's always the question of access. You were lucky, for a man with a duffle bag and no passport. The doctor in charge wanted to practise his English on you. What do you think of my English? I'm sure it's improving, thanks to you.

Harte: I can leave then, I guess. Today? Tomorrow?

Nurse: I thought you might speak a little Thai. Or Hindi, perhaps.

Harte: Just English. Well, a bit of parlez-vous français.

Nurse: Ah. Français. Nous pourrions peut-être, tenir cette conversation en français.

Harte: A bit. A few words. Bon jour. That's about it.

Nurse: I see. Well, English it is, then. *(Pause.)* Malaria, Mr. Harte. Such a nuisance of a disease. Did you know it was once induced as a cure for syphilis?

Harte: What?

Nurse: It's true. One of those things discovered by accident. The high fever caused by malaria killed the syphilis bacteria. Once the patient had been out of his head with the fever for a few days, they used quinine to cure him. No more syphilis. Of course this was a cure for the privileged. That goes without saying.

Harte: So if I had syphilis when I came in here—hypothetically speaking—I'd be cured now.

Nurse:	Accidentally cured. I suppose you would be. You were out of your head, I can attest to that. And quite a talker too. On and on about the rattle of bones or some such thing.
Harte:	The rattle of bones?
Nurse:	Well, never mind. None of it made much sense.
Harte:	But I'm back to normal now, eh? Right as rain.
Nurse:	I wouldn't exactly say that. Still, we need the bed. We always need the beds. I'll be back shortly with your ice water. Oh. I almost forgot. *(Pulls a letter from his pocket.)* This is for you.
Harte:	For me?
Nurse:	The original postmark is old, but it's from Canada. Addressed to you in Fiji.
Harte:	Fiji? I haven't been in Fiji for years.
Nurse:	Everyone's talking about it, imagining this letter following you around, trying to catch up to you. The tortoise and the hare, and the tortoise finally caught the hare sleeping, or sick as a dog in this case.
Harte:	It can't be for me. You might as well take it back.
Nurse:	Read the return address.
Harte:	Can't make it out.
Nurse:	Here. Let me see. *(Takes the letter and reads.)* Marguerite Waker. Box 211. St. James. Sask-at-chew-an. Canada. There. You see?
Harte:	Marguerite Waker.
Nurse:	You do know her, then. Family? A sister?
Harte:	I don't remember. You might as well take it with you.
Nurse:	Here. Think about it.

He puts the letter on the bed.

You're not well enough, Mr. Harte, to be travelling alone, living out of a suitcase, as you say in English. If you want me to contact someone…

Harte: There's no one.

> *The nurse exits. Harte stares at the letter and finally picks it up, turns it over and over, reads the return address to himself.*

Marguerite Waker. It should say, Mrs. Charlie Waker. Or Mr. and Mrs. Charlie Waker. *(Pause.)* Charlie. Christ, not Charlie.

Scene 3

> *Ruben is waiting. He's got a couple of old suitcases, and a few cardboard boxes tied with string.*

Ruben: *(Reading a sign, slapping at the odd mosquito.)* Welcome to St. James. Welcome. Who's welcome? Everyone? Are you going to welcome every Tom and Dick and Harry who steps off the bus? You ought to think about that. You ought to qualify it.

> *Marguerite enters and approaches Ruben with trepidation. They haven't seen each other for a long time.*

Marguerite: Hello, Ruben.

Ruben: Marguerite.

Marguerite: How are you?

Ruben: Never mind me. How about you?

Marguerite: I'm all right. Getting by.

Ruben: And Joel. How's Joel?

Marguerite: As well as can be expected.

Ruben: I should have been here for the funeral, but I got…

Marguerite: You don't have to explain.

Ruben: I didn't know how long you'd need me so I brought a few things.

Marguerite: I see.

Ruben: Extra things. Just in case. I apologize for not getting here sooner, Marguerite. When you called to tell me about…with the bad news…

Marguerite: About Andrew. You can say it. I'm not made of glass.

Ruben: About Andrew. Yes. I should have told them then and there I was taking time off, should have said, "I'm gone. This is family, my sister's boy." That's what I should have done.

Marguerite: It doesn't matter. No one was expecting you.

Ruben: Oh. Well, then. *(Pause.)* It's not easy to get away when you're management, you know. I told you about the promotion, didn't I? When you called?

Marguerite: There's no sense standing here in the street. Let's get your things in the car.

Ruben: Right. So Joel's okay then, is he? All things considered.

Marguerite: I'm hoping he'll find himself a job for the summer. I've rented out most of the land. There's not much for him to do at home.

                Ruben tries to lift one of the boxes and he seems to have no strength. He loses his balance.

Ruben: Damn.

Marguerite: What's the matter?

Ruben: I'm having a little back trouble. Nothing serious.

Marguerite: Back trouble?

Ruben: Pulled something the other day.

Marguerite: Here. Let me then.

Ruben: Nothing worse than a bad back, eh?

Marguerite: I've never had a bad back.

Ruben: Man's most common complaint.

Marguerite: The car's just around the corner.

Ruben: Marguerite.

Marguerite: What?

Ruben: I want to do whatever I can to help out.

Marguerite: Look. Let's get something straight. You and I both know that you would never travel halfway across the country just to help me out. I don't know why you're here, the real reason, but I'm sure I'll find out sooner or later.

Ruben: There's no reason except…

Marguerite: *(Interrupts.)* Don't insult me.

Ruben: Maybe I shouldn't have come.

Marguerite: And don't play games with me. I'm not going to let you get away with anything. Not anything.

Ruben: I can see you haven't changed much.

Marguerite: No. And I don't imagine you have either.

Ruben: *(Pause.)* I'm anxious to see Joel. All grown up now, I guess, eh? How big's he? Six feet? Sports nut, I'll bet. What's he like? Football? He play football?

> *Ruben tries to pick up one of the suitcases but he doesn't have the strength.*

Marguerite: Are you sure it's just your back?

Ruben: What's that supposed to mean?

Marguerite: I can get these. You just get yourself to the car.

> *Ruben slaps at a mosquito.*

Ruben: Mosquitoes are bad, eh?

Marguerite: About like usual.

Ruben: I forgot about the damned mosquitoes.

> *Marguerite exits with the bags. Ruben takes a flask out of his pocket, takes a drink.*

Welcome to St. James. Ah, Beauty, I might live to regret this.

> *Ruben follows Marguerite.*

Scene 4

Harte is sitting on the edge of the hospital bed, packed and ready to go. The letter is open. Harte studies a photograph, then reads the letter. When he's partway through the nurse enters and watches him.

Harte: *(Reading.)* "Dear William. Or perhaps I should call you Cap. Charlie always called you Cap, short for Captain I understand, but I don't know why. There must be a story. This is a difficult letter for me to write. I know how close you and Charlie were, and I thought you would want to be informed that he passed away a week ago yesterday as the result of a farming accident. The doctors tell me he died instantly with no suffering, so that is a blessing, if there is a blessing to be found anywhere in this. You grasp at straws. Our boys, Andrew and Joel, are too young to really understand what has happened, but they'll miss Charlie and I will try to keep his memory alive for them. I don't know what else to tell you. I hope this letter reaches you. I am sending it to the last address we have for you. Perhaps we'll meet some day in happier times. All the best to you. Sincerely, Marguerite Waker." *(Pause.)* Charlie. Christ.

Harte folds the letter and exits.

Nurse: Now there's someone you can call.

Scene 5

Much later the same night. Ruben is passed out in a chair. Joel starts pounding on his drums (off stage). The noise wakes up Marguerite.

Marguerite: Judas Priest. Joel? Joel, stop that right now. Stop it and get in here. Ruben, wake up and go to bed. Ruben. Ruben! *(She shakes him. He's dead to the world.)* Oh, for… *(To Joel.)* Is anyone else out there? Is Stevie there? If she is, it's time you got her home. Joel!

She picks up a bell, like a dinner bell, and rings it. Ruben still doesn't stir.

Marguerite: Joel!

The drumming stops.

Thank you. Thank you very much. Now if Stevie's there, take her home. If she isn't, get in here right now. Joel. Answer me.

Joel: She isn't here. And I'm not coming in.

Marguerite: Don't be ridiculous.

Joel: I'm sleeping out here.

Marguerite: In the garage.

Joel: Yes.

Marguerite: Stevie's there, isn't she?

Joel: I said she isn't here.

Marguerite: Judas Priest.

More drums, silence. Joel enters.

Joel: Fine. I'll sleep in the house. If that makes you happy. Whatever makes you happy. *(Sees Ruben.)* Who the hell is that?

Marguerite: Your Uncle Ruben. You've been drinking, haven't you?

Joel: I had a few beers. Big deal. Uncle Ruben. Where did he come from?

Marguerite: I don't know where he came from. He's here for a visit. I don't know how long he's staying.

Joel: He doesn't look so bad. He doesn't have horns, at least not that I can see.

Marguerite: That's enough of that. You were driving, weren't you?

Joel: If I want to be an asshole it's up to me, isn't it? What difference does it make to you? I don't see why it should matter to you.

Marguerite: You didn't used to do this. Drinking and staying out half the night, driving around the countryside. That was Andrew's trick.

Joel: Andrew's trick. I like the way you phrase that.

Marguerite: Are you trying to be like him? Is that it?

Joel: Why would I want to be like Andrew? He's dead.

Marguerite: And you're going to end up dead too if... This is for my benefit. It's all for my benefit.

Joel: It's my life.

Marguerite: Do not do this to me.

Joel: Sorry.

Marguerite: I'll do something drastic. I'll...I'll turn you in. That's what I'll do. Next time you go anywhere in that car, I'm phoning the police and I'm going to tell them to stop you. I'm going to tell them to take away your driver's license. Do you hear me? I will. I swear I'll do that.

Joel: I said I was sorry. Okay?

Marguerite: All right.

                Joel starts to exit, then he stops.

Marguerite: What? *(Pause.)* Joel? What's wrong?

Joel: You won't understand.

Marguerite: I'll try. I promise.

Joel: Everything's wrong. School's a big waste of time. I don't want to go.

Marguerite: It'll feel strange for a while. Your friends probably aren't sure what to say to you. Anyway, the year is almost over. Just a few more weeks.

Joel: The teachers pretend they're all sympathetic because of Andrew, but what they really want to say is, one more year to get it together, you'd better pull your socks up because everything depends on next year, the rest of your life depends on it, screw up and your life is down the toilet. Well, I'm not interested in school and I wish people would just leave me alone.

Marguerite: Joel, honey…

Joel: Don't call me honey. I'm not a kid.

Marguerite: I realize that.

Joel: I'm an adult.

Marguerite: You're almost an adult.

Joel: I'm old enough to get married.

Marguerite: What?

Joel: I want to get married.

Marguerite: What?

Joel: That's right. You heard me.

Marguerite: You're not serious.

Joel: I am.

Marguerite: You're seventeen years old, for God's sake. You can't be serious.

Joel: Well, I am.

Marguerite: I knew this would come to no good. I knew you shouldn't be dating a girl older than you. She might be ready for marriage, but you're just a boy….

Joel: I'm not "just a boy," for Christ's sake. And it's my idea. Stevie doesn't know yet. I haven't asked her.

Marguerite: She's pregnant.

Joel: No! I just…want to get married. I figure we can move in here, and…and just live here. We can both live in my room. Stevie can help you out. With the house and stuff.

Marguerite: I don't need help with the house.

Joel: Well, whatever. There's room for us here. The house is practically empty now.

Marguerite: My God. You need counselling. This is not normal.

Joel: Normal? What is normal anyway? *(Referring to Ruben.)* Is he normal?

Marguerite: I don't know.

Joel: He's drunk as a skunk.

Marguerite: He most certainly is not.

               Joel picks up an empty bottle from the chair.

Marguerite: Oh my God.

Joel: Do you think he's come to be a good role model for me? A positive male influence?

Marguerite: *(Shaking Ruben.)* Ruben. You wake up this instant, Ruben. Ruben!

Joel: I'm not changing my mind, you know. I'm old enough to make up my own mind.

               Joel exits.

Marguerite: Ruben! Wake up right now.

               Ruben opens his eyes.

Ruben: My car.

Marguerite: What?

Ruben: Where's my car?

Marguerite: I haven't a clue.

Ruben: What have you done with the 'Vette?

Marguerite: Ruben!

Ruben: Beauty.

Marguerite: Ruben, wake up right now.

Ruben: Beauty?

Marguerite: Beauty? Oh for… *(Exits in disgust.)*

Ruben: Christ.

Scene 6

Harte is in a hotel lobby somewhere in Thailand, trying to make a phone call. His duffle bag is at his feet. The person at the hotel desk doesn't speak English. There is a large exotic potted plant on the floor.

Subtitles appear as the clerk speaks.

Harte: Phone. I want to make a phone call.

Clerk: *(Looking at him suspiciously. In English.)* Telephone?

Harte: Long distance. Yeah. Telephone.

Clerk: *(In his own language.)* [You want to make a telephone call?]

Harte: That's right. I want to call long distance. Can you get me a long distance operator? An international operator?

Clerk: [You want to use the telephone?]

Harte: Do you speak English? I need someone who speaks English.

Clerk: *(In English.)* No English. *(In his language.)* [You can use the phone. As long as you pay the charge. How will you be paying?]

Harte: Long distance. International call. Canada.

Clerk: [Ah. Canada. You'll need an international operator.]

Harte: Canada. That's right. Canada.

Clerk: [Do you have a calling card?]

Harte: Pardon? What?

Clerk: [Calling card. Let me have your calling card.]

Harte: Cash. I'll pay cash. *(Shows him his money.)*

Clerk: [I'll try to get you an international operator. But they're not always available. *(Dials.)* Hello? *(Pause.)* An international operator, please. *(Pause.)* Canada. *(Pause.)* I see. *(Pause.)* I see. Thank you very much

	then. *(Hangs up.)* There's no operator available. Gone for lunch. You'll have to try again in half an hour.]
Harte:	What?
Clerk:	[Half an hour. Try again.]
Harte:	You don't understand. This is an important call.
Clerk:	[I'm sorry, I don't understand you. Can you speak a little Hindi? Thai? Urdu? Even a little would help.]
Harte:	There's been a death. I'll pay you extra if you can get me through. See? I'll pay. Just tell me how much.
Clerk:	[That won't do you any good. You'll have to wait. Try again in half an hour.]
Harte:	This is hopeless. Well, never mind. It's probably a stupid idea anyway.

He starts to leave but then he sees the plant on the floor. He picks it up and turns back to the clerk.

	I want to send some flowers. See? Flowers. Where can I wire flowers?
Clerk:	[What? Put that plant down right now. Put it down.]
Harte:	Flowers. You know. Like this. Plants. Flowers. Where can I wire some flowers?
Clerk:	[You cannot have that plant. Absolutely not. Now put it down or I'll call security.]
Harte:	There must be some place. Just give me directions.
Clerk:	[Why would I let you have that plant? Do you think I'm crazy? Now get out of here. I knew you were trouble the minute you walked in.]
Harte:	Look. It's simple. I want to wire flowers. There's been a death.
Clerk:	[Security! Security! There's a foreigner out here trying to steal a plant.]
Harte:	Why are you shouting? Calm down, for Christ's sake.

Clerk:	[Get out. Shoo. Shoo. Security!]
Harte:	*(Putting the plant down.)* All right, all right. Don't have a coronary.
Clerk:	[Out. Away with you.]
Harte:	Christ.
	He exits.
Clerk:	[You see all kinds.]

Scene 7

Joel is eating breakfast. Ruben enters in a bathrobe. He has his flask in his pocket. He pours himself some orange juice, adds liquor from his flask.

Ruben:	Morning. You must be Joel.
Joel:	Yeah.
Ruben:	*(Holding out his hand.)* Ruben. Your Uncle Ruben.
Joel:	*(Ignoring his hand.)* My uncle? This isn't one of those things where your mother brings a man home and you're supposed to call him uncle, is it? Nah. Couldn't be.
Ruben:	Kind of a joker, eh? Your dad was kind of a joker. Maybe you get it from him.
Joel:	I guess I must.
Ruben:	So. Do you remember me?
Joel:	Should I?
Ruben:	I thought you might remember the time I took you to…
Joel:	*(Interrupts.)* Nope. Don't remember that.
Ruben:	Well, maybe you were too young. *(Pause.)* There was the time I came for Christmas and brought you…
Joel:	*(Interrupts.)* Don't remember that either.

Ruben: You must remember that.

Joel: Nope. Don't remember you at all. Are you sure you're my uncle? I don't remember Mom talking about any uncle. Except the one…you couldn't be him.

Ruben: Yeah. That's me. That must be me.

Joel: The skeleton in the family closet?

Ruben: You're a regular clown, aren't you? Must be something in those Cheerios.

Joel: So where'd you come from?

Ruben: None of your business.

Joel: What are you doing here?

Ruben: What do you think? I came for a visit. To see you and your mother.

Joel: I guess you know about Andrew.

Ruben: Of course I know about Andrew.

Joel: I guess you know he was drunk, then. When he died.

Ruben: Well, yeah. Your mother told me that.

Joel: Rolled the car. Stupid bugger. Anyway, I wouldn't let her catch you with that.

Ruben: What? This? Oh, I get it. You thought… It's orange juice.

Joel: No kidding. Not that I'm against it, personally. You might think, because of Andrew, that I'd be against it, but I'm not. I mean, personally, I wouldn't object if you were to pass it this way.

Ruben: What?

Joel: Pass it on over here. Come on. No one will know but us.

Ruben: Get out.

Joel: Come on. We're just two guys here, right?

Ruben: Yeah. You're right. Two guys.

                Ruben passes the flask. Joel splashes booze on his Cheerios.

                So. I guess it's hard for you here with just your mother, eh? I mean, men have to stick together. Women don't get it, do they?

Joel: Get what?

Ruben: Things. They just don't get it. Women. Boy. Sometimes I…well, you know what I'm talking about.

Joel: I don't have a clue.

Ruben: Sure you do. And like I said, we men have to stick together.

                They hear Marguerite coming.

Ruben: *(Snatching the flask back.)* Jesus. Why didn't you tell me she was here?

                Marguerite enters from the garden.

Joel: You didn't ask.

Marguerite: Have you seen my hat, Joel? That sun is going to be hot today.

Joel: How should I know where your hat is? It's not like I borrow it.

Marguerite: I see you two have met.

Ruben: Yeah. We've met. Cute kid.

Marguerite: Did you get Uncle Ruben some breakfast?

Joel: He's doing okay on his own. He found the orange juice.

Marguerite: *(To Ruben.)* As you can see, you're going to have to help yourself around here. Do you want some cereal? The bowls are in the dishwasher.

Ruben: Ah, no thanks, I'm not a breakfast kind of person.

Marguerite:	What in the world does that mean? By the way, Joel, when I went for the mail this morning I noticed a sign in the window at the Co-op. They need some part-time help. I told Mr. Kerley you'd be calling him.
Joel:	What'd you do that for?
Marguerite:	Because I think a job would be good for you. What will you do this summer if you don't have a job?
Joel:	I'm not going to waste my time packing stupid groceries.
Marguerite:	You have better things to do with it, I suppose.
Joel:	I could die tomorrow. I don't want to say the only thing I did with my life is pack groceries.
Marguerite:	You're not going to die tomorrow. Now I want you to phone Mr. Kerley. If you don't, I'll do it for you. Ruben, will you please eat something?
Ruben:	I haven't eaten breakfast in thirty years.
Marguerite:	All right, fine. Starve. Just don't blame it on me. *(Pause.)* You wouldn't believe what I heard in town this morning. *(Pause.)* Is anyone interested?
Joel:	If I have to be.
Marguerite:	Howard Sealey is apparently trying to grow some kind of fruit trees on my land. Apricots, I heard from one lady. Grapes, someone else said. I even heard pineapples. Imagine. You have to feel sorry for the man. I wonder if it's Alzheimer's.
Ruben:	Who the hell is Howard Sealey?
Marguerite:	I doubt if you'd remember him. He's a local...what would you call him?
Joel:	Geezer.
Marguerite:	Eccentric. Anyway, after his wife died his family moved him into an apartment in town, so I let him work a patch of garden in the north pasture.

Ruben: And he's growing fruit trees out there.

Marguerite: So they say. But obviously it's not true. A nice man,
              though. He did love his garden. It must have killed
              him to give up the yard.

              Joel drinks the milk that's in the bottom of his bowl.

              Joel, when are you going to stop doing that? One
              minute you're telling me you want to get married and
              the next you're...

Joel: *(Interrupting.)* I knew you'd bring that up. I never
              should have told you.

Marguerite: I'm glad you told me. Now I can make sure it doesn't
              happen.

Joel: As if it's up to you.

Marguerite: I'm your mother.

Joel: You're going to keep bringing it up now, aren't you?
              Every time I turn around, you're going to be...

Marguerite: *(Interrupting.)* It's on my mind. And don't drink the
              milk from your cereal bowl. It's rude. Isn't it, Ruben?

Joel: How would he know?

Marguerite: He's an adult. Anyway, I just hope Mr. Sealey doesn't
              start dragging people out here. I don't want the whole
              gardening club traipsing through the yard. But
              probably not. I can't imagine anyone taking him
              seriously.

              Joel is about to leave.

Marguerite: Where are you going?

Joel: I don't know. Somewhere.

Marguerite: I was hoping you'd help me in the garden today.
              Things are starting to come up, including the weeds.

Joel: Get him to help.

Marguerite: Joel.

Joel: He's got nothing better to do.

Ruben: I'd like to do that for your mother, but I've got this
             little back problem…

Joel: Back problem! I don't think so.

Marguerite: What has got into you?

Joel: He's a drunk.

Marguerite: Joel!

Joel: You know it as well as I do. Check the pocket of his
             robe. One thing about him. He's a generous drunk.
             He's willing to share.

             Joel exits.

Marguerite: What did he mean by that?

Ruben: What was that about Joel getting married? The kid's
             got some girl knocked up?

Marguerite: No, he doesn't. And if he meant what I think he
             meant…

Ruben: Jesus. What do you take me for?

Marguerite: Why are you here, anyway?

Ruben: What?

Marguerite: You heard me. Let's get to the point. Why are you
             here?

Ruben: Okay. That's fair. The point. *(Pause.)* I know I didn't
             do my share in the past, Marguerite, but I thought I
             could make it up. I'll do whatever you want me to do
             around the place. I can be a handy-man. And help out
             with Joel. I can see he's a handful.

Marguerite: I don't need your help. Let's get that straight right
             now.

Ruben: I have a lot of holiday time coming.

Marguerite: I suspected that you were planning to park yourself.

Ruben: It won't be easy for them. I've been there a long time.
             Corporate memory and all that. I didn't leave a phone

number. I figured they'd be calling me all the time, and I didn't want them bothering you. Not now. At a time like this.

Marguerite: I won't turn you away. You're my brother. But there are conditions.

Ruben: Conditions?

Marguerite: How are you fixed, financially?

Ruben: What kind of question is that?

Marguerite: Do you still own property on the coast?

Ruben: Too much upkeep. I sold it.

Marguerite: Right. And you sold your car too?

Ruben: My car?

Marguerite: You arrived here without a car.

Ruben: I didn't sell my car.

Marguerite: Then why did you come on the bus?

Ruben: My car needed a little work. I didn't want to take it out on the highway.

Marguerite: I know why you're here, Ruben. You came home because you're sick. You're sick and you're broke.

Ruben: What are you talking about?

Marguerite: You ran when it was father, but you can't run now. So here you are.

Ruben: Is that what you're talking about? Father?

Marguerite: I want the truth, Ruben. We both might as well accept it.

Ruben: Okay. All right. *(Pause.)* I can see how you might assume, because of father, that I... How you might think... Christ, I don't know if I can say this.

Marguerite: You're going to have to, sooner or later.

Ruben: It's not what you think. I have...a drinking problem.

Marguerite: A drinking problem.

Ruben: And I came here to...

Marguerite: *(Interrupting.)* I can see that you have a drinking problem, but that's not what...

Ruben: *(Interrupting.)* Hear me out. You asked for the truth, now hear me out. You're right, I didn't just come to help you. I do want to help, but I came to get away from work, the pressure and...

Marguerite: Stop it.

Ruben: So I admit it. That's the first step, right? I'm an alcoholic.

Marguerite: It's not just the alcohol.

Ruben: Go ahead... Call me a drunk, I can take it. My name is Ruben McDonald and I'm a drunk.

Marguerite: There's more, and you know it.

Ruben: What do you want from me, for Christ's sake?

Marguerite: You know what I want.

Ruben: You just can't cut me a break, can you? You want me to spill my guts all over the floor. Okay, Marguerite. If that's what you want. If that's what you're asking me to do. *(Pause.)* If Charlie were alive...

Marguerite: *(Interrupting.)* I don't want to talk about Charlie.

Ruben: No, wait. If Charlie were alive, you two would be together. Together and happy. There's no doubt in my mind. No doubt at all. But me...I don't know. Me and women. So that's it. I'm a loser. A number-one, first-rate loser. There. Now are you satisfied?

Marguerite: So what exactly are you telling me, Ruben?

Ruben: Before I came here, I was...with someone.

Marguerite: A girlfriend.

Ruben: Beauty.

Marguerite: What?

Ruben: Her name was Beauty.

Marguerite: Beauty? Oh, for…

Ruben: That's her name. Her mother took one look at her and called her Beauty.

Marguerite: No one calls a baby Beauty. Unless it's a horse. That's what people call their horses.

Ruben: It's her name. And I came here to…to recoup, to get over... well, you know.

Marguerite: Your broken heart.

Ruben: That's right.

Marguerite: Oh, for…you are hopeless. Hopeless.

Ruben: Life, eh? The things it dishes out.

Marguerite: All right, Ruben. You and I both know that neither alcohol nor "Beauty" is your biggest problem. But for now, here's the deal. You are not allowed to drink in my house.

Ruben: I can lick it.

Marguerite: Or on my porch, or in my garden, or anywhere on my property. Are you prepared to abide by that? You'd better think carefully.

Ruben: I said I was going to lick it. That's my plan. That's why I'm here.

Marguerite: I have a very vulnerable son to think about, and I will think about him first, so help me God. Are we in agreement?

Ruben: Yes.

Marguerite: All right then. And don't imagine it will be easy.

Ruben: No sweat.

Marguerite: There will be no compromise.

Ruben: I'm counting on you.

Marguerite exits.

(Calling after her.) I think this back thing is just about gone. Another day or two and I'll be able to help you out in that garden. A day or two won't make a difference, I don't imagine.

Scene 8

A flower shop in Thailand. Harte is trying to have flowers wired to Marguerite. The vendor can't speak English.

Subtitles appear as the vendor speaks.

Vendor: [Good afternoon. Can I help you?]

Harte: I want to send some flowers. Sympathy flowers.

Vendor: [Excuse me?]

Harte: *(Gesturing dead.)* Funeral flowers. Sympathy.

Vendor: [Ah, funeral flowers. I'm so sorry. Who is it that has passed away? A close family member? Or a dear friend, perhaps?]

Harte: Sorry. No speak...whatever. Does anyone here speak English? English?

Vendor: [No English here. But I can help you. I'm very understanding and have impeccable taste when it comes to sympathy flowers. Now, who are the flowers for? A man? A woman?]

Harte: I want to send funeral flowers. Do you understand?

Vendor: [How much money would you like to spend? We have flowers to suit all pocketbooks. As long as you have a pocketbook, we have flowers.]

Harte: Christ, it's a good thing I'm not coming in here to tell you your shop is on fire. Okay. Let me see. Stick to basics. Flowers. Funeral. Canada. Get it?

Vendor: [Canada. You'll want to wire, then. And how will you be paying?]

Harte:	That's right. Flowers to Canada. Now we're getting somewhere.
Vendor:	[AMEX, perhaps? VISA? EnRoute? We take most cards.]
Harte:	No credit card. I'll pay cash. *(Shows his cash.)* Money. How much?
Vendor:	[Ahh. Cash. I see. Well, now we can proceed, at least. All right, then. What kind of flowers would you like? Your choice for Canada is going to be limited. Roses and chrysanthemums, I suspect.]
Harte:	A sympathy arrangement. It's got to be…you know, dignified. Not too colourful. Sombre.
Vendor:	[Do you have a colour preference? I believe there is a particular colour denoting sympathy in North America. White, perhaps?]
Harte:	What? This is hopeless.
Vendor:	[This is difficult, but we can get it right. Let me see. White? Should we go with white? Or maybe white is for weddings. Oh, dear. You wouldn't want to make a mistake.]
Harte:	Doesn't anyone else work here? Someone who can speak English? Hello?
Vendor:	[Sir. Please keep your voice at a respectable level.]
Harte:	Anyone? English?
Vendor:	[There is no need for making a scene. The language barrier is a problem for you westerners, I know, but we're doing fine.]
Harte:	*(Picking up a fantastic bouquet of exotic flowers.)* These. Understand? I want flowers sent to Marguerite Waker, Saskatchewan, Canada.
Vendor:	[You want those flowers?]
Harte:	Like this. A bouquet. An arrangement.

Vendor: [That is not the way it works. You can imagine what those flowers would look like by the time they arrived. Not to mention that it is illegal to send plants across international borders.]

Harte: Sometimes I swear I'm not living in the twentieth century. Twentieth century, get it? We should all be speaking the same language by now.

Vendor: [I am beginning to dislike your tone of voice.]

Harte: English is the universal language. If we all spoke English, no problems. What do think of that, eh?

Vendor: [You have made yourself quite clear. You are an unpleasant and disagreeable foreigner.]

Harte: (Grabs a piece of paper and writes.) Marguerite Waker. St. James, Saskatchewan, Canada. There. (Holds out a fist full of money and points to the flowers again.) How much?

Vendor: [For these particular flowers...this exact arrangement...quite a lot.]

Harte: Take it. I'll be penniless, but what the hell.

Vendor: [I'm only too happy to relieve you of your money. But not all of it. I'm not the sort to leave a man destitute. Even someone like you.]

Harte: Now, you see that Marguerite Waker gets flowers. I'll be checking, do you hear?

Vendor: [I believe our transaction is complete. I've enjoyed our discussion immensely, but please don't feel you have to linger.]

Harte: I'll be checking.

Vendor: [Very good.]

            Harte exits.

Vendor: [These exact flowers. Yes. I'll see what I can do. (Weighing the flowers in his hands.) A gift. Perhaps that will work. (Writing.) A gift for Marguerite Waker, St. James, Saskatchewan, Canada. Wherever that is.]

Scene 9

Two weeks later.

Ruben is rummaging in one of his bags. He pulls out a bunch of empty rum bottles, and then one with a bit left in it. He gets a glass of ice and Coke, then sits in a plastic lawn chair and pours the last of his booze into his glass. He stares at his empty bottle.

Mr. Sealey approaches, pulling a wagon with a big water tank on it. He's singing "Cool Water." He sees Ruben.

Mr. Sealey: Oh. Hello there. I wonder if Marguerite...Mrs. Waker...is here.

Ruben: Nope.

Mr. Sealey: I see. Well. You would be Mr. McDonald?

Ruben: That's right.

Mr. Sealey: The one who came on the bus.

Ruben: How'd you know that?

Mr. Sealey: Two weeks ago, I believe it was.

Ruben: Whole town must be talking about it.

Mr. Sealey: Oh yes. People love to talk. It can be a problem.

Ruben: So you must be the gardener. The orchard man. Mr. Sealey.

Mr. Sealey: Hard to keep a secret around here. Like I said, it can be a problem. But it's not my biggest problem, as I'm not much for keeping secrets. No. Not my biggest problem. Do you want to know what that is?

Ruben: What?

Mr. Sealey: Water.

Ruben: Water.

Mr. Sealey: That's right. Dry as a bone this year.

Ruben: You can say that again. It's enough to make you cry.

Mr. Sealey: A desert, that's what this country really is.

Ruben: A desert.

Mr. Sealey: Scientists confirm it. People who know. Some of them think we ought to let the whole place grow back to cactus and buffalo grass, stop trying to fight with nature.

Ruben: There might be a grain of sense in that.

Mr. Sealey: Possibly. But nature isn't perfect either. There's always a thing or two you can improve on. I see Marguerite's garden is up.

Ruben: I don't know what the hell she grows. Lot of work if you ask me.

Mr. Sealey: I don't like the look of Marguerite's garden. Don't like the look of it at all.

Ruben: What's wrong with it?

Mr. Sealey: Don't know. Does she irrigate?

Ruben: Irrigate? I couldn't tell you.

Mr. Sealey: Take fruit trees. If you're going to expect any yield at all, you have to irrigate.

Ruben: What kind of fruit trees are we talking here anyway? Rhubarb?

Mr. Sealey: Rhubarb, Mr. McDonald, is not a tree. It is an herbaceous perennial. Fond of moisture, yes, but resilient. Now, apricots are another matter altogether. No question, regular soakings are required. And that's my problem, Mr. McDonald. Marguerite's north pasture is a challenge in that regard.

Ruben: Apricots.

Mr. Sealey: You came from British Columbia, I understand.

Ruben: Where'd you hear that?

Mr. Sealey: Your bus driver was my neighbour's second cousin. He told her that your ticket originated in British Columbia. He couldn't remember the exact location, but he thought it was somewhere in the Okanagan.

Ruben: Jesus.

Mr. Sealey: She plays the piano, my neighbour does. I hear her playing through the walls. They're thin, you know, apartment walls. Not like a house. I had a very good house, but…well, never mind. *(Pause.)* Perhaps you know something about growing fruit trees.

Ruben: Me?

Mr. Sealey: If you're from the Okanagan.

Ruben: I'm not, and I don't know a damned thing about fruit trees.

Mr. Sealey: Oh. I am disappointed. I was hoping…well, I knew the chance would be remote, even if you were from the Okanagan, but I was hoping you would be a fruit grower. Or perhaps an itinerant worker.

Ruben: The itinerant part is right, but I don't know anything about fruit.

Mr. Sealey: Well, then. I'll just have to do the best I can, without your anticipated expertise. I'm very pleased to have met you, Mr. McDonald.

Ruben: Same.

Mr. Sealey: How long will you be staying?

Ruben: How long? I don't know. I'm not sure. As long as Marguerite needs me, I guess.

Mr. Sealey: Good. Glad to hear that. A good woman. Doesn't deserve what she's had to go through.

Mr. Sealey moves off, pulling his wagon.

Ruben: Mr. Sealey? Howard, isn't it? Can I call you Howard?

Mr. Sealey: Of course.

Ruben: Howard, you're not a drinking man are you?

Mr. Sealey: Me? Don't touch it. Not a drop.

Ruben: Oh. Well, that's good. Just checking. Wouldn't want anyone keeping a still out on Marguerite's property.

Mr. Sealey: A keen sense of humour, I see.

Ruben: That's me. A laugh a minute. Ha ha.

Mr. Sealey: A still. That's a good one.

>   *Mr. Sealey exits singing "Cool Water."*

Scene 1ð

>   *Harte is trying to call Marguerite from somewhere in southern India. He's standing at a hotel desk again with a clerk across the counter from him. The clerk does not speak English.*

>   *Subtitles appear when the clerk speaks.*

Clerk: [Your call is going through.]

Harte: What's that?

Clerk: [We've got through to Canada.]

>   *The clerk hands Harte the phone, but Harte seems reluctant to take it.*

Clerk: [You'd better take it. Quickly. It could be difficult to get another line.]

Harte: Hang up. I've changed my mind.

Clerk: [We're lucky to have got through.]

Harte: *(Taking the phone.)* Christ. What do I say?

>   *Marguerite's phone rings. Ruben stares at it, but doesn't answer it.*

>   *Joel enters.*

Joel: Hey. Aren't you going to answer the phone?

Ruben: No.

Joel: Why not?

Ruben: It's...it's a wrong number. Yeah.

Joel: How do you know?

Ruben: Been getting them all afternoon. Ought to call the phone company. Complain.

Joel: It might be Stevie.

Ruben: It's a wrong number.

Joel: You don't know that.

Joel tries to pick up the phone. Ruben stops him.

Ruben: Don't answer it.

Joel: Why not?

Ruben: Never mind why not. Just do as I tell you.

Joel: Are you crazy or what? It might be for me. It might be important.

Joel tries to push Ruben out of the way and Ruben falls over.

               Jesus. What's the matter with you anyway?

Ruben: Nothing's the matter with me.

Joel: You can't even stand up.

Joel grabs the phone.

Joel: Hello.

Harte hears him, but doesn't answer.

Joel: Stevie?

Harte hangs up.

Joel: She hung up.

Ruben struggles to his feet.

Ruben: Piss off, kid. Get the hell out of here.

Joel: It's my house.

Ruben:	I said, piss off. Go on. Get out of here.
Joel:	Why the hell wouldn't you answer it? You're crazy. Crazy as a shithouse rat.
	Joel exits.
Harte:	*(To the clerk.)* Wrong number. It was a wrong number.
Clerk:	[Was this an important call? A business call, perhaps?]
Harte:	Thanks. I'll try again later.
Clerk:	[Not a business call. A personal call.]
Harte:	Do you speak English?
Clerk:	*(In English.)* No English.
Harte:	Of course not.
Clerk:	*(In his own language.)* [That look of disappointment...it must be personal. Personal, yes. Very definitely.]
Harte:	Tell me this. If you had an old friend and he died, say fourteen years ago, but you just found out, would you call his widow, a woman you'd never met? Would it be right, after all that time?
Clerk:	[How long since you've spoken with her?]
Harte:	After all those years, there's a pretty good chance she wouldn't remember who you were.
Clerk:	[Do you want me to try again? The call?]
Harte:	And if she did remember, you might remind her too much of the past, old memories, things she'd closed the book on.
Clerk:	[I can tell you this with absolute conviction. Absence makes the heart grow fonder, but only to a degree. Then it's the opposite.]
Harte:	Fourteen years. That's a hell of a long time.
Clerk:	[You're in love. Poor man. It's written all over you.]
Harte:	She could be remarried.

Clerk:	[Forgive me, but I'm a romantic. An incurable romantic. I'm crazy about American movies.]
Harte:	Or she could be there alone.
Clerk:	[The thought of two people in love.]
Harte:	That's what Charlie was afraid of.
Clerk:	[Imagine seeing her again.]
Harte:	Well. That's it, then, isn't it? There's the answer to my question.
Clerk:	[Holding her in your arms.]
Harte:	But a phone call, that's hardly adequate. A beginning, maybe, but hardly the fulfillment of an obligation.
Clerk:	[Kiss her cherry red lips. Feel her heart beating next to yours.]
Harte:	It could be complicated, given my current situation.
Clerk:	[Go. Go. Run to her.]
Harte:	Airline tickets. Passport problems.
Clerk:	[It brings tears to my eyes.]
Harte:	But passports and airline tickets can be acquired. There's another complication.
Clerk:	[You're going to her, then?]
Harte:	*(To clerk.)* What the hell are you going on about?
Clerk:	[To your sweetheart? Your soul mate?]
Harte:	What?
Clerk:	*(Gesturing beating heart.)* [Sweetheart. Sweetheart.]

> *Harte grabs the clerk and pulls him so they're face to face.*

| Harte: | Look here. It's not as simple as that. She has a family. She's a mother with two boys. Look at me and what do you see? |
| Clerk: | [My friend, the eleventh hour is not the twelfth hour.] |

Harte: Oil and water.

Clerk: [You're choking me.]

Harte: Now that's a problem. Oil and water.

Clerk: [You can let me go now, if you don't mind.]

Harte: *(Letting him go.)* Sorry. No harm intended. Sorry.

Clerk: [You're a very passionate man.]

Harte: *(Giving him money.)* I...thanks for your help. You've been helpful. The phone call.

Clerk: [No, no. That's not necessary.]

Harte: Take it. Take it. *(Leaving.)* Oil and water. But you don't find out unless you give it a shot.

Clerk: *(Calling to Harte.)* [Remember, no problem is too great for lovers. *(To himself.)* Two people, apart—couplets without rhyme, bees without honey, planets out of orbit. But together, everything falls into place—synchronicity, poetry, sublime happiness. I live to think about falling in love.]

Scene 11

> *Ruben's eyes are closed. Marguerite enters with a package and a box of ice cream in a grocery bag.*

Marguerite: Ruben. Wake up.

Ruben: Huh? Oh. I was just resting my eyes.

Marguerite: I have a very interesting package here. And I haven't a clue who it's from.

Ruben: For me?

Marguerite: No. Why would it be for you?

Ruben: Are you sure?

Marguerite: It's addressed to me. Postmarked Thailand.

Ruben: Thailand? It's not for me, then. Even Beauty couldn't get that far away.

Marguerite: There's a shipping label here. Says it's a gift. A gift from
              Thailand. How strange.

Ruben: Who do you know in Thailand?

Marguerite: Nobody.

Ruben: Open it.

              *She does. It's the flowers from the flower shop, only now
              they're rotted and mouldy.*

Marguerite: Smells a little musty… Oh, my God.

Ruben: What the hell is it?

Marguerite: I'm not sure.

Ruben: It's flowers, I think. Was flowers, I should say.

Marguerite: Flowers.

Ruben: Christ almighty. Look here. There's a card, but it's
              falling apart, you can't read it.

Marguerite: Where did these come from?

Ruben: Well. Someone obviously heard about Andrew. Must
              be sympathy flowers.

Marguerite: Who sent them?

Ruben: I don't know. Is there a return address?

Marguerite: No.

Ruben: Give them here. I'll get rid of them.

Marguerite: Someone travelling. Maybe a friend of Andrew's.
              Some young man travelling somewhere.

Ruben: Who would send flowers in the mail?

Marguerite: They're ruined.

              Marguerite cries.

Ruben: Hey. Marguerite. Don't. Don't cry…

Marguerite: They were lovely once.

Ruben: Yeah. Just…Jesus…I hate it when women cry.

Marguerite: You can tell they were lovely flowers.

Ruben: I'll get rid of them. Give them here.

             Marguerite holds them away from Ruben.

Marguerite: A young man…a boy…wouldn't know that flowers don't last…you can't send flowers in the mail…a boy wouldn't know that, would he? What do boys know about things like flowers?

Ruben: Give them here, Marguerite. I'll throw them out.

Marguerite: No.

Ruben: They're rotten.

Marguerite: They're from a friend of Andrew's.

Ruben: You don't know that.

Marguerite: Flowers for Andrew. You don't expect young men to be that thoughtful. Like the waiter who blew in Mrs. Rorke's ear on the cruise ship. Who would expect a young man to be that thoughtful?

Ruben: What? Look. You're in shock, Marguerite. You've had some kind of relapse, some kind of post-traumatic…whatever. Give those to me. I'll throw them out, and then I'll…I'll make some tea.

Marguerite: Keep away.

Ruben: And…and tomato soup. Is there any tomato soup in the house?

Marguerite: Don't touch them.

Ruben: Marguerite.

             Joel enters.

Joel: What's going on?

Marguerite: We've got flowers. More flowers. From a friend of Andrew's. The one who's in Thailand.

Joel: What?

Marguerite: Andrew has a friend in Thailand, doesn't he? Didn't I
              hear him say that? What's his name? You know, Joel.

Joel: Where the hell's Thailand?

Marguerite: Doesn't he?

Joel: What's she talking about?

Ruben: It's a mistake. Give me the flowers. I'll throw them
              away.

Marguerite: *(To Joel.)* You can't think of anyone, a friend travelling
              in Thailand?

Joel: No.

Ruben: Look for tomato soup in the cupboard, Joel. I think
              your mother needs a bowl of soup.

Joel: Soup?

Marguerite: Tea.

Ruben: What?

Marguerite: I could use a cup of tea.

Ruben: Give the flowers to me.

              She does.

Marguerite: I'm sure they were lovely.

Ruben: Yeah.

Marguerite: I don't know who could have sent them.

Ruben: It's a mistake. We'll get it sorted out.

Joel: What's going on?

Ruben: Nothing. Just make some tea.

              *Ruben takes the flowers, digs a hole in the garden and
              buries the flowers.*

Joel: I hate it when people say nothing. Something's going
              on. Tell me what.

Marguerite: It's all right, Joel. I bought some ice cream in town.
              Let's all have ice cream with our tea.

Joel: Is something wrong?

Marguerite: I just need a little holiday, that's all. But it's the wrong time of the year, isn't it? The garden's just coming up. The sun's shining. Winter is when you should take a holiday. Maybe this winter I'll try it. I'll go on a holiday. Someplace warm. Ruben will be here. The two of you could manage.

Joel: Ruben will be here? What do you mean? I thought he was leaving.

Marguerite: I think he'll be here...well, for quite a while.

Joel: How long is quite a while?

Marguerite: You remember Grandpa...how he was before he died. I think Ruben...you've seen how weak he is, he has no strength at all...

Joel: What are you saying? That Ruben has whatever Grandpa had? And he's staying here? Until he dies? No way. He can't stay here.

Marguerite: I'm not positive, but... Anyway, he can help out. And if I go on a holiday, you wouldn't be here on your own.

Joel: I wouldn't be here on my own anyway.

Marguerite: What do you mean?

Joel: You know what I mean. Stevie and I are getting married. I'm going to marry her.

Marguerite: Oh, for...

Joel: We don't need him. What did he ever do for you anyway? Nothing. He took off when Grandpa got sick and you did everything.

Marguerite: You are not going to marry that girl. You're too young.

              She exits.

Joel: You're going to have to get used to this, you know. You might as well get used to it.

              Ruben comes back in.

Ruben: Where's Marguerite?

Joel: It's going to happen, whether you like it or not.

Ruben: Where's the tea? Did you put the tea on like I told you?

Joel: I don't do what you tell me.

              Joel exits.

Ruben: Where did everyone go? What did I say? *(Picks up the ice cream.)* The ice cream's melting. Marguerite? What should I do with this ice cream?

              Ruben exits with the dripping ice cream.

Scene 12

              Mr. Sealey crosses the stage carrying a roll of chicken wire and a pair of wire cutters. He stops and looks at Marguerite's garden. He sniffs the air and examines the plants.

Mr. Sealey: Very strange. A vegetable garden ought to be an improvement on nature. One would think so. But not always. Apparently not. Quite a mystery, I must say.

              Mr. Sealey exits.

Scene 13

              A dark and seamy little bar in Bombay. Harte is seated at a table doing business with a stranger. They share a bottle. The man speaks English. He has a very well-organized briefcase, with many pockets containing maps, passports, airline tickets, etc.

              About halfway through this scene we see Mr. Sealey digging in the soil.

Man: So, it's travel arrangements you're interested in.

Harte: *(Slaps at a mosquito.)* That's right.

Man: Where is it you want to go?

Harte: Canada.

Man: Canada. That shouldn't be too difficult.

          He reaches across the table and feels Harte's forehead.

          You don't look very well. You seem to be running a fever.

Harte: It's this damned climate. The heat and the humidity.

Man: It's difficult to get used to. But one does get used to it, if one is here long enough.

Harte: I've been here forever and I'm still not used to it. I won't be here much longer, though, if you can get me to Canada.

Man: It's certainly cooler there, from what I've heard.

Harte: Yeah. So what can you do for me?

Man: I don't mean to pry, but for my own interest, why aren't you going the more...shall we say, conventional route? A proper travel agent.

Harte: I prefer to travel budget.

Man: I see. How budget are we talking?

Harte: If you were in the car rental business, we'd be talking rent-a-wreck.

Man: I see.

Harte: There's also the problem of a passport.

Man: What problem is that?

Harte: I don't have one. I'm not a citizen of any country. I don't exist.

Man: It seems you've come to the right person.

Harte: Look. Let's forget the casual conversation. Can you help me or not?

Man: You see this briefcase? This briefcase contains the answers to all your travel problems. It can get you anywhere and international borders are of no concern. Unless…

Harte: Unless what?

The man pulls a knife from the briefcase and holds it to Harte's throat.

Harte: Hey!

Man: Unless I smell deceit. Who sent you?

Harte: No one. I just want a cheap ticket.

Man: I'm in a dangerous business and I have to take precautions, particularly with my western customers, who think they own the world.

Harte: I don't own anything.

Man: You could disappear here, just like that, and no one would notice the Earth is no longer blessed with your presence.

Harte: Believe me, I know that. Honest to Christ.

Man: You forget, I'm not likely to be a Christian. *(Releasing Harte.)* I'll be frank. My willingness to help you depends on what you have in your pocket.

Harte: I've got money. Not a lot, but enough, I hope.

Man: Let me see it.

Harte takes out what's left of his money.

Harte: Here. You can have it all.

Man: *(Taking the money.)* You expect me to get you to Canada for that?

Harte: I was hoping.

Man: Wishing would be a better word. Hoping implies that there is at least a slight possibility for success. Wishing on the other hand…well, you can wish for anything. You can wish for great wealth. You can wish you were king. You can wish for happiness, when there isn't a hope in hell. Do you see what I mean?

Harte:	Have you got a ticket for me or not?
Man:	Let me see your watch.
Harte:	I don't own a watch.
Man:	Any other jewellery? A wedding ring?
Harte:	No watch. No wedding ring.
Man:	Anything of value?
Harte:	No.
Man:	*(Putting the knife, the bottle and Harte's money in his briefcase.)* I'm afraid you're out of luck.
Harte:	You can't help me?
Man:	I'm a businessman, not a social worker.
Harte:	What about my money?
Man:	I charge an hourly rate.
Harte:	You son-of-a…
Man:	The drink was complimentary. It's part of my service.
Harte:	God damn it, I want my money back.

Another man suddenly approaches the table.

At the same time, Mr. Sealey unearths a bone. He picks it up and studies it.

Man:	My friend. So nice to see you again. I hope luck has been on your side since our last…

The intruder lunges at the man. A fight ensues. Harte grabs the briefcase and runs. Blackout.

End of Act I.

ACT II

Scene 14

In the dark the audience hears the sound of a high performance car changing gears. The sound fades. The lights come up.

It's a few weeks later. Marguerite is sitting in a lawn chair, staring at her ailing garden. Ruben approaches, unwrapping a book from a brown mailing wrapper.

Marguerite: I see you found your mail on the counter.

Ruben: I ordered this book for you.

Marguerite: A book? What kind of book?

Ruben: A gardening book. Organic gardening. This is the new way to grow a garden.

Marguerite: How do you know about that?

Ruben: I heard the guy who wrote this book on the radio.

Marguerite: It's just a fad. Some theory city gardeners have come up with. I grow my garden the same way mother did, and it hasn't failed me yet.

Ruben: Pardon me, Marguerite, but I don't see any prize ribbons on whatever the hell you've got growing out there.

Marguerite: A book's not going to fix anything. It's got to be the year. The heat, and such heavy dew in the morning. It doesn't make sense.

Ruben: I thought maybe you could try some of this companion planting business. They say if you plant the proper things together they grow better. Look here. Radishes and carrots. You plant the seeds in the same row. The radishes come up first and break the ground for the carrots. After the radishes are done, you pull them out and there's room for the carrots to grow.

Marguerite: You don't know anything about gardens, Ruben. You don't know what you're talking about and neither does that book.

Ruben: Compost. There's a whole chapter here on compost. Everyone's doing that now, eh?

Marguerite: Not a good idea, if you ask me. It attracts rats.

Ruben: Hummm. It says here your soil should contain living compost...living compost? What a concept. Jesus.

Marguerite: Let me see that.

Ruben: Got you interested, eh?

Marguerite: I'm not interested. I'm...curious.

Ruben: *(Hands her the book.)* Anyway, I thought there might be some tips in there. And like I said, I heard the guy on the radio. He has to have some kind of credibility if he gets on the radio.

Marguerite: You ordered this for me, you said?

Ruben: Yeah.

Marguerite: Well. Thank you.

Ruben exits.

Ruben: Thought you might want to read it.

Marguerite flips through the book.

Scene 15

Joel is pounding on the drums in the garage. Ruben enters.

Ruben: Hey. Joel. *(Drums pound.)* Joel! I said hey. Hey there!

Joel: *(Stops drumming.)* Hey, Ruben.

Ruben: So. Practising, eh? *(Pause.)* So. Where's the rest of the band?

Joel: This is it.

Ruben:	Just you?
Joel:	Yeah. The guitar player left town. You know how it is. Bands break up. Interpersonal problems. Fights over artistic control.
Ruben:	I see.
Joel:	That's why most bands break up, you know. Even the great ones.
Ruben:	Like Lennon and McCartney.
Joel:	Who?
Ruben:	The Beatles.
Joel:	Yeah. Like them. Keep it simple. That's the secret.
Ruben:	I see your point. You ready to take a break?
Joel:	A break?
Ruben:	You've been out here a long time. You must be ready for a break.
Joel:	No.
Ruben:	Come on. It'll be my treat.
Joel:	What do you mean?
Ruben:	Well, I thought you could…you know, take a little trip into town. Get yourself a…a soda at the cafe.
Joel:	A soda? You've got to be joking.
Ruben:	I'll give you the money. You deserve a break.
Joel:	No.
Ruben:	No?
Joel:	I don't want to go to town.
Ruben:	Why not?
Joel:	I just don't.
Ruben:	I'd appreciate it if you'd pick a little something up for me.

Joel: I told you. I don't want to go to town. *(Pause.)* You can go. Take the car.

Ruben: I don't think so. I've still got this bad back.

Joel: You can't drive anymore, can you?

Ruben: What?

Joel: That disease. Whatever you've got. Mom says you can't drive because of it.

Ruben: What are you talking about? What disease?

Joel: The one Grandpa had.

Ruben: I don't have…Jesus H. Christ. What's she going around telling people? I don't have any damned disease.

Joel: That's what she told me.

Ruben: Well, that's ridiculous.

Joel: She also said you'd try to talk me into taking you to town, or picking up booze for you.

Ruben: Let's communicate man to man here. Now, you know what it's like to want a few drinks. There's no harm in it, as long as you know how to limit yourself. I can do that now. Your mother's been good for me. But there are things she doesn't understand. Black or white, that's how she sees it. Sober or drunk, you got to be one or the other. Am I right?

Joel: You might be, but that doesn't mean I'm doing you any favours.

Ruben: I'll pay you twenty bucks. Just drive into town and get me a bottle of rum.

Joel: I'm not old enough. They won't sell me a bottle of rum.

Ruben: All kids know how to get booze.

Joel: Why should I do you a favour? You're nothing to me.

Ruben: I'm your uncle, your blood relative.

Joel:	Some blood relative.
Ruben:	What do you mean by that?
Joel:	You know what she told me? When Grandpa got sick and needed help, you took off. Then Dad died and she did all the work, and you didn't call or write or anything.
Ruben:	I was out of the country.
Joel:	Sure you were.
Ruben:	I was out of the country. What was I supposed to do?
Joel:	Now you've got the same thing Grandpa had and it serves you right.

Joel exits.

| Ruben: | You come back here. You can't talk to me that way. Your mother didn't raise you like that. Joel! |

Scene 16

Lights come up on Harte trying to make a phone call again. He has a blanket draped over his shoulders. He's in Karachi, Pakistan. He uses a calling card from the briefcase, which is open at his feet. An international operator comes on the line. The audience hears her voice.

Harte:	Hello? I'm still here.
Operator:	I'll just confirm the number, sir. Area code 306-722-9837.
Harte:	That's it.
Operator:	Could I have your calling card number, sir?
Harte:	407-000-6355-8992
Operator:	Your call is being connected.

Marguerite's phone rings.

| Harte: | Okay. Here we go. *(Rings.)* Oil and water. *(Rings.)* Give it a shot. |

Marguerite answers in her robe. It's the middle of the night.

Marguerite: Yes.

Harte: Operator?

Marguerite: Who is this?

Harte: It's...maybe I have the wrong number.

Marguerite: You ought to be more careful at three in the morning.

Harte: Yeah. Wrong number. Must be.

Marguerite goes to put the phone down, then changes her mind.

Marguerite: Who were you trying to reach? *(Pause.)* Hello.

Harte: Uuhh, Mrs. Waker. Mrs. Charlie Waker.

Marguerite: This is she. Who's calling? *(Pause.)* Oh for...Who's calling?

Harte: Marguerite?

Marguerite: Yes. Now, who is this?

Harte: I'm...an old friend of your husband.

Marguerite: A friend of Charlie's?

Harte: That's right.

Marguerite: What friend of Charlie's?

Harte: He knew me by a nickname. Cap. But you won't remember. It's been too long.

Marguerite: Short for Captain.

Harte: That's right.

Marguerite: Harte.

Harte: That's right.

Marguerite: The given name...

Harte: Cap. Cap is good enough. Look Marguerite. How can I put this? I know my timing is off, but I just heard. I don't know what to say. I'm sorry. That's all I can think of.

Marguerite: Well. Sorry is enough.

Harte: I've been trying to call, but the lines...let's just say it's not quite the twentieth century over here.

Marguerite: Where are you calling from?

Harte: Karachi.

Marguerite: Where?

Harte: Pakistan. Karachi, Pakistan. Other side of the world. *(Pause.)* Marguerite? Are you still there?

Marguerite: Yes. I was just wondering... Pakistan. Imagine. Well, Charlie said you'd spend your life travelling. I guess he was right. Are you still in the merchant marine?

Harte: No. Not for years. Marguerite, the thing is, I've got an opportunity, and I made a promise to Charlie, a long time ago, I know, but would you mind...? I was wondering if you'd mind if I came for a visit. A quick visit. I wouldn't stay long.

Marguerite: A visit? Here? Come all the way from Pakistan?

Harte: This opportunity...

Marguerite: *(Interrupts.)* Please. Do come. It's been a long time since Charlie... I would be so glad to see you.

Harte: You would?

Marguerite: Of course. A friend of Charlie's is always welcome.

Harte: Really?

Marguerite: He talked about you often. You know, there's a photograph of you and Charlie. I'm sure of it. You and Charlie... I don't remember where, but you're standing in front of a statue. A famous statue somewhere.

Harte: No kidding.

Marguerite: I'll have to try and find that photograph. Put a face to the voice.

Harte: I don't imagine I'll look much like the man in the picture. Lot of water under the bridge.

Marguerite: Yes, well, that old devil time.

Harte: I have a photograph of you.

Marguerite: Of me?

Harte: And Charlie and the boys. The one you sent in the letter.

Marguerite: Letter?

Harte: When Charlie passed away.

Marguerite: I enclosed a picture? It's guaranteed not to be a likeness. Not anymore. *(Pause.)* You know, I'm wondering…someone sent me flowers recently. From Thailand. I couldn't read the card so I don't know who sent them. Could it possibly have been you?

Harte: Flowers? You know, I did try to wire flowers, but I didn't think you'd get them. The language problem.

Marguerite: I did get them.

Harte: I'll be damned. Were they…I mean, I didn't choose them. When you wire flowers you take a chance. I hope they were all right.

Marguerite: They were fine. Thank you. They were lovely.

Harte: Good.

Marguerite: It was thoughtful. So, when can I expect you to arrive?

Harte: Who was it that said, "If you come to a fork in the road, take it?" That's what I'm doing. Taking the fork. So I can't quite say when I'll get there. Marguerite?

Marguerite: Yes?

Harte: I'm glad I called. I wasn't sure, but…well, I'm glad I called.

Marguerite: It was very good to hear from you.

Harte: I'll be seeing you, then. Before too long, I hope.

Marguerite: I look forward to it.

> *They both hang up.*
>
> *Harte closes the briefcase. He begins to shiver and pulls his blanket around himself.*
>
> *Marguerite stares at the phone.*
>
> *Joel's drums start up in the shed.*

Marguerite: Oh for... Joel! Joel, stop that and get in here right now. It's the middle of the night.

> *She rings her dinner bell. The drums stop. Joel enters.*

Marguerite: Don't do that in the middle of the night, Joel. You should know better. *(Pause.)* Have you been drinking again?

Joel: No, I haven't. And if I was, it wouldn't be any of your business. You aren't in charge anymore, not when it comes to my life. I'm old enough to make my own decisions.

Marguerite: You're old enough to make stupid decisions. I've seen the evidence of that.

Joel: Stupid decisions, like what?

Marguerite: You know what I'm talking about.

Joel: You mean Stevie.

Marguerite: That's right. Getting married is not going to help. It's going to complicate your life, and hers, and that's all it will do.

Joel: Complicate my life. Well, you're right there. She's complicated my life, that's for sure.

Marguerite: What do you mean?

Joel: I asked her. Tonight.

Marguerite: This is not right.

Joel: Next week, I said. Let's get married next week. As soon
             as we can get a license. And I bought her a ring. See.
             Seven ninety-five at Wal-Mart. Genuine glass…

Marguerite: You've got another year of high school, for God's sake.

Joel: Well, you don't have to worry, because she said no.

Marguerite: She said no?

Joel: And then she told me she's leaving. Yeah. She doesn't
             want to get married because she's decided to go back to
             school. University in Vancouver. To study science.
             Astronomy or some damned thing.

Marguerite: School. Well, that's good. Good for her.

Joel: We can be engaged, then, I said. I've got this ring here,
             this genuine glass diamond. And she said no to that
             too. It doesn't have to be any big commitment, I said.
             It's a ring from Wal-Mart, for Christ's sake. You could
             at least wear the ring. But no. She didn't want it at all.
             She gave it back to me. She insisted that I take it.

Marguerite: She has to think about her future, Joel. School is a good
             thing for Stevie. She's a smart girl. You know that.

Joel: Why didn't she take the ring? She could have at least
             taken the ring.

Marguerite: She knows marriage is not something to joke about.

Joel: I wasn't joking. *(Pitching the ring.)* Anyway. Fuck her.
             I don't care if I ever see her again. And you don't have
             to act all sympathetic, because I know you're glad. You
             can't deny it.

Marguerite: No. I'm not going to. When is she leaving?

Joel: I don't know. Soon. A couple of days. Some relative
             got her a job in Vancouver. It starts as soon as she can
             get there.

Marguerite: Well. That's good. Good for her.

Joel: That's good?

Marguerite: Yes. You're too young, far too young to be thinking about marriage, both of you.

Joel: So we should go our separate ways and never see each other again?

Marguerite: You'll meet someone else and…

Joel: *(Interrupting.)* Someone else? I don't want anyone else. Jesus. What is wrong with you?

Marguerite: Joel. There's no need…

Joel: Don't talk to me anymore. Don't say one more word.

             Joel exits.

Marguerite: What's the use? Just what is the use?

Scene 17

Marguerite is in the garden, mystified by its failure to thrive.

Mr. Sealey is standing at a podium of some kind. There might be a banner on the podium saying "Horticultural Society."

Mr. Sealey: Friends and neighbours, members of the Horticultural Society, I'd like to thank you for allowing me to speak to you this afternoon, for giving me the floor. I'll begin with the sunflower. The sunflower. Native to the Americas, peculiar in its tendency to lean toward the sun. *(Quoting.)* "…it casteth out the greatest flowers,…for it is greater than a great Platter or Dishe…it showeth marveilous faire in Gardines." From an old book—*Joyfull Newes out of the New-Found Worlde. Wherein are Declared the Rare and Singular Vertues of Divuers Herbs, Trees, Plants, Oyles & Stones.* By Mr. Nicolas Monardes, an explorer and a scientist in his own right. Perhaps you've read it? No. Of course not. Well. I'll just get on with it and…and show my slides. Let's see. How do you work this?…never was much good with machines. There we go. Could someone turn the lights down? Thank you. Thank you very much.

Slide of a huge sunflower in bloom comes on the screen.

I'll begin with this one. Now, as you may know, I name my best sunflower each year after someone that I admire. This one is my 1985 sunflower, and I called her Betsy after my wife. *(Chokes up.)* My wife is departed now, as most of you know. You remember my wife Betsy, don't you? Fine woman. Fine woman. Miss her terribly. Excuse me.

Slide of another sunflower, even bigger than the first.

Now this one, I grew this a few years back, 1990, I believe it was. Won me a number of prizes including a brand new hundred dollar bill. Diana, I called her, after the Princess of Wales. A fitting tribute, as it's turned out. Who would have guessed? Such a tragedy.

Slide of a huge sunflower, maybe eight feet tall with a two-foot diameter head. Mr. Sealey is standing in front of it, grinning.

Now this one...this one was last year's pride and joy. And I've named it after an illustrious member of our community. Mrs. Marguerite Waker, who has been so kind as to allow me free reign on a small section of her property. Which brings me to what I really wanted to talk to you about this afternoon. I know you've heard rumours about my experiments...very sound, scientifically speaking. Add a little faith and determination and you can work miracles. What I'm talking about is the future of fruit production. Yes, fruit. To be specific, apricots. *(Pause.)* I thought some of you might be interested in my work. I'm willing to share secrets. After all, I won't be here forever, will I? A committee perhaps. A core of dedicated volunteers. *(Pause.)* No? No one? No volunteers? Well. To be expected, I suppose. A doubting Thomas in every crowd, or a crowd of doubting Thomas's, as the case may be. Thank you all very much.

He exits.

Scene 18

Joel is pounding on the drums. Ruben enters. Joel stops.

Ruben: Hey. Joel.

Joel: Hey, Ruben.

Ruben: So what did you want to talk to me about?

Joel: I might be ready to deal.

Ruben: Yeah?

Joel: That's right.

Ruben: Okay. Let's not beat around the bush here. You've heard of "scratch my back and I'll scratch yours." If you've got something for me, then you want something in return.

Joel: Maybe.

Ruben: So let's get this show on the road.

Joel starts banging on the drums again.

Hey. I said, Hey!

Joel stops.

Don't fuck with me, Joel. I'm a desperate man. You know that. Now what do you want? Just tell me and we can strike a deal.

Joel: I want money.

Ruben: How much?

Joel: Lots.

Ruben: Lots? What does a kid need lots of money for?

Joel: I'm saving for university.

Ruben: University. Right. How much, then?

Joel: Forget it. It was a stupid idea.

Ruben: How much?

Joel: You're broke. If it wasn't for us, you'd be dying in some crummy hotel somewhere.

Ruben: You insolent little prick.

           Ruben starts toward Joel but his legs give out and he falls.

Joel: Ruben? Uncle Ruben?

Ruben: Get away. Get away from me.

Joel: Are you hurt?

Ruben: Leave me alone. And stop treating me like I'm a damned geriatric case. I just tripped on the extension cord. Everybody trips once in a while, especially in a mess like this. All these…what are all these cords for anyway? Christ, I need a drink. And if anybody in this family had any compassion he'd buy me a bottle of rum. That's my drink. Dark fucking rum. But there you go. Your mother's got her almighty high standards, and you…well, like I said, you're an insolent little prick. So that's that.

           Ruben goes to leave. Joel pulls a bottle of rum out from somewhere.

Joel: Here. Take it.

Ruben: What's this?

Joel: What do you think it is? Take it. I was going to give it to you anyway. I just thought you might have enough money for… I want out. There's no life here, just day after day, the same thing. What am I supposed to do? Hang around and year after year, the same thing? Jesus, I'd rather be dead.

Ruben: Don't say that.

Joel: I'm not planning to kill myself. That's not what I mean.

Ruben: Just don't…say that.

Joel: *(Pause.)* So what is this disease you've got?

Ruben: What disease?

Joel: I have a right to know. I've got the same genes as you, at least some of them.

Ruben: If you're talking about the disease your grandfather had, forget it. It's not hereditary. It was…a virus. Anyway, even it was hereditary, you couldn't get it.

Joel: How's that?

Ruben: Your mother obviously doesn't have it, so how could you?

Joel: Your understanding of genetics is pretty impressive. I don't know why they aren't paying you big bucks at the research station in town.

Ruben: You know, for a kid, you've got a lot of bad karma.

Joel: Who are you to talk?

           Ruben picks up the guitar and twangs. He can't play much.

Ruben: How do you play this thing, anyway?

Joel: Don't touch that.

Ruben: Why not? The guitar player left, didn't he? You said he left. He won't care.

Joel: Put it down. *(Pause.)* I said, put it down.

Ruben: This guitar player, the one who left. He probably couldn't play much. I mean, how many kids can? You all want to be rock stars, but how many of you can really do anything? I imagine your guitar player was just another loser kid who couldn't play his way out of a wet paper bag.

Joel: Fuck you, Ruben.

Ruben: *(Stops playing.)* You really want to hit somebody, don't you, Joel? You want to beat the living crap out of somebody. Well, come on, then. I'm your man.

Joel: I don't know what you're talking about.

Ruben: That guitar player couldn't play worth shit. You're good to be rid of him.

                Joel lunges at Ruben.

Joel: You bastard. You son-of-a-bitch.

                They scuffle. Ruben falls over. Marguerite enters. Joel and Ruben scramble.

Marguerite: What's going on?

Ruben: Nothing. I tripped.

Marguerite: Are you hurt?

Ruben: No. It's nothing. I tripped on these...these damn extension cords. The kid was trying to help me up. Here, Joel. Give me hand. Help me up here.

                Joel does. Marguerite sees the bottle and picks it up.

Marguerite: What's this? What's going on here? Where did you get this?

Joel: Leave him alone.

Ruben: I've been thinking, and I figure we went about this the wrong way. I figure just a little drink now and then to take the edge off...

Marguerite: *(Interrupting.)* Who bought this for you?

Ruben: I'm sick, Marguerite. I've got to have a drink.

Marguerite: Answer me right now.

Ruben: Just who do you think you are, anyway? You're not a doctor. This isn't the Betty Ford. You don't have clue about this. You could kill me.

Marguerite: Who bought this liquor? I want to know right now.

Joel: I did. I bought it.

Marguerite: You did?

Joel: And it was my idea, so leave him alone.

Marguerite: All right, Ruben. I'll do it.

Ruben: You'll do what?

Marguerite: I'll keep you in liquor. So that you'll leave Joel out of it.
              And if I find out that you have given Joel one drop...

Joel: *(Interrupting.)* I said it was my idea.

Marguerite: ...you will be on that bus and gone. Do you hear me?

Ruben: I hear you.

Marguerite: And there's another condition too.

Ruben: What?

Marguerite: I insist that you use a cane.

Ruben: A cane?

Marguerite: That's what I said. I'll pick one up for you from the
              Home Care office in town.

Ruben: I won't use it.

Marguerite: You're going to hurt yourself, Ruben. One of these
              days you are going to fall and hurt yourself.

Ruben: This is blackmail, Marguerite. Blackmail.

Marguerite: You can take whatever steps necessary to make things
              easier for yourself, or you can continue to deny that
              you've had the misfortune of inheriting a bad gene.

Joel: See. It is hereditary.

Ruben: Forget it. I might be desperate, but I'm not that
              desperate. I will not use a cane.

Marguerite: Those are my conditions.

Joel: I could get it, couldn't I? I could have it right now.

Marguerite: You remember what I said about Joel.

              Marguerite hands Ruben the bottle and exits.

Ruben: *(Calling after her.)* Fine. You want a crippled up old
              invalid, I can give you that. I can arrange that.

Joel: She doesn't care.

Ruben:	I'll rot in bed. I'll rot in bed before I'll hobble around on a God damned cane.
Joel:	She doesn't even care.
Ruben:	What are you going on about?
Joel:	That disease. I could have it and she doesn't even care.
Ruben:	Of course she cares. And quit whining. You're the guy with the whole big exciting world ahead of you. Isn't that what you were trying to tell me earlier? That you're not going to let the world pass you by?
Joel:	Well, yeah.
Ruben:	Quit whining, then.
Joel:	I'm not whining. I'm just frustrated. I have no money.
Ruben:	What do you expect? You're a kid. Kids don't deserve to have money. What have you done to deserve it?
Joel:	Me? What have I done? What about you?
Ruben:	I don't deserve anything and I haven't got anything. *(Pause.)* You ought to straighten up this mess. All these damn cords. Someone could get hurt.
Joel:	*(Pause.)* You know the guitar player?
Ruben:	Yeah.
Joel:	It was Andrew.
Ruben:	I know that. He was good, was he? Kind of a legend.
Joel:	That's right. A legend. Anyway, it's no big deal. Someone dies, no big deal. It just happens.
Ruben:	It is a big deal. You don't have to pretend it's not. *(Pause.)* The girlfriend. I hear she…turned you down.
Joel:	Who told you that?
Ruben:	You know who.
Joel:	Yeah, well, I hear you got dumped too.
Ruben:	Good news travels fast.

Joel:	*(Pause.)* Stevie's in Vancouver.
Ruben:	So I heard.
Joel:	Where's this famous "Beauty"?
Ruben:	Don't know. Same place as my car. Yellow Corvette. Classic. 1963. God, I loved that car.
Joel:	We're both a couple of losers, eh?
Ruben:	Maybe it's in the genes. Hey. Just joking. Just joking, kid.

> *The audience hears the sound of the car again.*

Scene 19

> *Mr. Sealey crosses the stage carrying the bone. He stops and looks like he might be about to call Marguerite, then he looks at the bone and carries on.*

Scene 20

> *Marguerite is in her kitchen with a pile of lettuce leaves. She checks each leaf, and then drops it in a slop bucket. Ruben can be seen in bed. From the looks of his bed, he's moved into it.*

Joel:	Is he ever going to get up?
Marguerite:	You're one to talk.
Joel:	You know what I mean. He hasn't been out of bed for a week.
Marguerite:	He says he has the flu.
Joel:	It's that disease, isn't it?
Marguerite:	If stubbornness is a disease, then yes. He's got it in spades.
Joel:	So is he going to die or what?
Marguerite:	I don't know, Joel. I don't know what's going to happen. What are you looking for?

Joel: Tylenol.

Marguerite: It's probably in Ruben's room. Have you got a headache?

Joel: Sort of. I'm not feeling very well.

Marguerite: Maybe you're getting the flu.

Joel: Yeah. Maybe. Do you think I'll get that other thing?

Marguerite: What other thing?

Joel: That disease.

Marguerite: I've told you before, Joel. I've been tested. I'm not a carrier. *(Pause.)* Look at these lettuce leaves. Have a look.

Joel: They look fine to me.

Marguerite: What do they smell like to you?

Joel: I don't want to smell them.

Marguerite: Rotten potatoes. Like a root cellar that's been left after the warm weather.

Joel: Yeah, well. I don't know anything about gardens.

                 Joel sees the photograph of Harte. Picks it up and looks at it.

Joel: Is this him?

Marguerite: Who?

Joel: This guy in the picture. Is this the guy who's coming?

Marguerite: I think he's coming. We'll see.

Joel: If he's a friend of Dad's he must be pretty old, eh?

Marguerite: Not that old.

Joel: Too old to be…like, travelling around.

Marguerite: What are you getting at?

Joel: I just wonder what he's doing. If he was my age, I wouldn't wonder. But if he's old, then it's weird.

Marguerite: I imagine he travels on business. Anyway, we'll find out, won't we?

Joel: A lot of people my age travel around.

Marguerite: Hardly. It costs money to travel.

Joel: Not that much. Depends how you live.

Marguerite: Just what are you getting at?

Joel: Maybe I'll go to the library.

Marguerite: The library?

Joel: Yeah. What's wrong with that?

Marguerite: Nothing. The library. That's good.

Joel: And I guess I'll stop and see Mr. Kerley about that job.

Marguerite: The job at the Co-op? I'm sure he's hired someone else by now.

Joel: I'll stop and see him anyway.

             Joel exits. Marguerite stares after him.

             Ruben has Marguerite's bell in the bedroom and he rings it.

Marguerite: What is it now, Ruben?

Ruben: I'm feeling a little peckish.

Marguerite: Maybe you should get up and get something to eat.

Ruben: Would you mind bringing me a bite? Just a snack. Don't go to any trouble.

Marguerite: I really think it would be better if you got up. You can't stay in bed the rest of your life.

Ruben: Cream of tomato soup. Whenever we were sick mother would fix Campbell's Cream of Tomato Soup. With dry toast. And maybe Jell-O chocolate pudding for dessert.

Marguerite: Your need to lie in bed is all in your head. It's time you got up and did something.

             The phone rings.

Ruben:	If that's for me...
Marguerite:	It is never for you. Face it, Ruben. You've managed to elude the mysterious Beauty.

> *Marguerite answers the phone. It's Harte. He's in Faisalabad. He has the briefcase and holds in his hand the picture of Marguerite's family. As he talks he wraps a blanket around himself. He shivers uncontrollably. As Marguerite talks, Ruben rings the bell. There is now a world globe near the phone.*

Marguerite:	Hello.
Harte:	Marguerite?
Marguerite:	Yes?
Harte:	Marguerite, it's Harte.
Marguerite:	William. It's William, isn't it? I've been trying to remember, and I think it's William. Am I right?
Harte:	William. That's right.
Marguerite:	I was pretty sure.
Harte:	So. How are you? How have you been?
Marguerite:	Fine. Just fine. Are you still in Pakistan? In Karachi?
Harte:	Karachi? No. That was...seems like years ago.
Marguerite:	Where are you now?
Harte:	Faisalabad.
Marguerite:	Where?
Harte:	Faisalabad. My travel arrangements are...well, let's say trying to get to Canada is like playing a board game.
Marguerite:	Where exactly is Faisalabad?

> *The bell tinkles.*

Harte:	Still in Pakistan. Look, Marguerite. I'm sorry it's taking me so long to get there, but I'm having a little trouble.
Marguerite:	What kind of trouble?

Harte: Schedules, airlines, passports. I'm trying to get a flight out of here, but I might have to take the train to Lahore.

Marguerite: I've heard travel can be complicated, not that I've experienced it first hand. I thought I might go on a trip a few years ago. I pored through travel brochures and even got my passport ready. But then, with the boys…well, it was too complicated. So, there you go. I have experienced the complications of travel, in my own way. Anyway, you can tell me stories when you get here.

Harte: Stories?

Marguerite: Travel stories.

Harte: Travel stories. Yeah. I have a few of those.

Marguerite: You can give me ideas. For where I might go, when I get the chance.

Harte: Marguerite…

Marguerite: Yes?

Harte: I'm afraid this might sound too familiar. Presumptuous. But when I think about you and your family, I realize that I'm…I'm a lonely man. I can't say I've experienced that before in my life. Loneliness. Or maybe I just didn't recognize it. Anyway, I just want to tell you how much I'm looking forward to seeing you and the family. Charlie's family.

Marguerite: Well. You and Charlie were like brothers.

Harte: That's right. Until we lost touch, and that was my fault. No one to blame but myself. I should have written. Or called. Marguerite…

Marguerite: Yes?

Harte: You don't know me. Showing up at your door… Are you sure it's all right?

Marguerite: Don't worry. We're famous for our hospitality around here.

Ruben's bell rings. She ignores it.

Harte: It's been fourteen years since Charlie passed away. Are you still...? You haven't remarried?

Marguerite: No. I haven't. And you? I assume you're a single man.

Harte: Single. Yes.

            Ruben's bell rings. Harte is apparently seized by stomach cramps. He doubles over and moans.

Marguerite: William?

            No answer. Ruben rings his bell again.

            Ruben. Stop ringing that bell. I'm on the phone. William?

Harte: Yeah. I'm still here.

Marguerite: I'm sorry. My brother...well, it's a long story. And this will be costing you a fortune.

Harte: Never mind that.

Marguerite: No, really. It can add up. It's so easy to lose track of time. But it's been good talking to you. I'm looking forward to your visit. Whenever you can get here. It doesn't matter.

Harte: Like I said, maybe I'll have better luck in Lahore.

Marguerite: Bye for now, then.

Harte: Yeah. Good-bye.

            Harte hangs up and pulls the blanket tightly around himself. Marguerite finds Pakistan on the globe. The bell tinkles.

Marguerite: You might as well quit ringing that bell, Ruben. You're sadly mistaken if you think you're getting your meals in bed. You can get up and join the world like the rest of us.

            Ruben's bell rings.

            I'm not kidding, Ruben. You can ring all you want but

room service is closed. The number has been disconnected.

Marguerite picks up lettuce leaves again. She smells them, then dumps the whole lot into a bucket.

Scene 21

Marguerite is in the garden, dumping the bucket and turning the lettuce leaves under. Mr. Sealey approaches from the direction of the orchard, pulling his wagon. He has a small basket of strawberries.

Mr. Sealey: Yoo hoo. Yoo hoo, Marguerite.

Marguerite: Mr. Sealey.

Mr. Sealey: I have something for you, Marguerite.

Marguerite: What's this?

Mr. Sealey: Strawberries. Not what you would call a bumper crop, but still, in these desert conditions, a success. A definite success. Take the basket. It's for you.

Marguerite: How nice.

Mr. Sealey: And there's more.

He pulls an apricot out of his bag.

An apricot. My first *prunus armeniaca*, as a result of a successful grafting experiment. Compatible scion and stock, firm union, an asexual means of reproduction, of course, but then you're not interested in all that. The important thing is that I've perfected the cut, my very own, the Sealey graft, and next year there will be more.

Marguerite: More...what?

Mr. Sealey: Why, apricots, of course. You must keep this a secret for now, Marguerite, to protect your privacy. I'll be writing it up eventually, and going to the research station, to the horticulturists. But for now, just you and me. What do you say? Our secret?

Marguerite: Are you telling me you grew this...this apricot...out somewhere in my north pasture?

Mr. Sealey: That is exactly correct.

Marguerite: Mr. Sealey, really, I don't believe this is possible. You're pulling my leg.

Mr. Sealey: It is possible. I've done it. Lovely blush, don't you think? Excellent aroma.

Marguerite: The strawberries, yes, but apricots...

Mr. Sealey: Imagine. Fruit stands beside the highway, and instead of signs saying "Fresh from B.C." we'll have "Locally grown." Locally grown. Imagine. And Marguerite...

Marguerite: Yes?

Mr. Sealey: The grapes are doing very well. Very well. I see the potential for a wine industry.

Marguerite: Wine?

Mr. Sealey: Fine wine. Now, promise me, you won't tell. Like I said, it's for your own protection.

Marguerite: You're asking me not to tell, when you've already told everyone in town, as far as I understand it.

Mr. Sealey: Yes, and I question my judgement on that, given the response I've had. But in future, if anyone asks, the strawberries came from the Co-op.

Marguerite: Of course. If anyone asks.

Mr. Sealey: Well, I must be off. Get this specimen home to the refrigerator. It will have to tested for eating quality. I do love a good apricot. *(Pause.)* There is one other thing. Perhaps you could help me with identification.

Marguerite: What is it?

He takes the bone from his wagon.

Mr. Sealey: I was digging around the roots, loosening the soil. One doesn't like to uncover ambiguous bones.

Marguerite: It's a deer, no doubt.

Mr. Sealey: A deer. Of course. I'm sure you're right. Well, that's a relief, knowing it's a deer.

Marguerite: That pasture is full of deer. Surely you've seen them. They're murder on fruit trees.

Mr. Sealey: I haven't, no, but I keep my trees protected. Chicken wire.

Marguerite: Ah yes. Chicken wire.

Mr. Sealey: Standard precaution. A deer. Well. It's unsettling to find a bone and not know what it belonged to, isn't it? Bones are a reminder, I always think. The sureness of death. When I found this bone, I thought, this was once a living thing, a particular creature, and now it's a bone. But it's not anymore, is it? Now it's a deer. That's something a little more specific than a bone. Oh, perhaps this is just my age. You can't deny the sureness of the destination, when you get up in years.

Marguerite: They go together, life and death. And there's not a thing we can do about it.

Mr. Sealey: Oh, my. I should have thought. So insensitive. Forgive me.

Marguerite: There's nothing to forgive, Mr. Sealey. Now, you'd better hurry along and get your prunus-whatever-you-called-it in the fridge.

Mr. Sealey: The fridge, yes.

Marguerite: Thank you for the strawberries. The Co-op always has good produce, don't you think?

Mr. Sealey: The Co-op? Oh, the Co-op, yes. Good produce. I agree. Absolutely. *(Leaving.)* An amazing woman.

Marguerite: *(When he's out of earshot.)* Amazing. Is that what I am?

Scene 22

Joel is by the phone with a pad of paper. Ruben is in bed.

Joel: Is there any mail for me?

Marguerite: No. What are you doing?

Joel: Nothing. You really get ripped off when you work, don't you?

Marguerite: I don't know. Why? What are you thinking?

Joel: Minimum wage. It's pathetic.

Marguerite: It's better than nothing. And you have no experience. You can't expect to earn a lot of money when have no experience. Not to mention education. What did Mr. Kerley say?

Joel: He's already hired someone.

Marguerite: That's what I thought. Well, there are other jobs. Did you try the service stations?

Joel: No.

Marguerite: That's a possibility. What are you figuring there?

Joel: Nothing much. Airfares.

Marguerite: Airfares? Just where are you planning to go?

Joel: Nowhere in particular.

Marguerite: To see Stevie, I suppose.

Joel: Yeah. To see Stevie.

Marguerite: The bus would be cheaper.

Joel: Not cheap enough. Nothing is cheap enough. Everybody rips you off. Like, the airlines don't even have student prices. Like only rich people can fly.

Marguerite: That's about it. Welcome to the real world.

Joel: Minimum wage. It's impossible. What kind of crap are you supposed to take, anyway?

Marguerite: If you're not prepared to start wherever you can and work your way up, you'll never get anywhere.

Joel: That's where you've got it backwards. You don't get anywhere if you put up with crap. Well, I'm not playing that game.

Marguerite: Good, Joel. Then maybe you should just go to bed like
Ruben, spend your life staring at the ceiling.

Joel: Fine. That's what I will do. It's better than putting up
with crap.

*Joel exits and flops on his bed. The audience can now
see both Joel and Ruben in bed. Ruben rings his bell.*

Marguerite: What is it, Ruben?

Ruben: My kingdom for a bowl of soup.

Marguerite: My kingdom for a maid. A cook. A gardener. And why
not a butler, a chauffeur, a waiter named Raoul? Why
not, indeed?

Ruben: Marguerite? Are you there?

Ruben rings his bell.

Marguerite exits.

Scene 23

The phone rings.

Marguerite: *(Off stage.)* Joel? Joel, can you get that? *(Pause.)* Joel?

Marguerite enters and answers the phone.

*Lights up on Harte. He's hot again and sheds clothing
as he talks. The audience sees Beauty, examining a
road map. Harte has a map of western Canada.*

Marguerite: Hello.

Harte: Marguerite. It's me. I've just landed.

Marguerite: William.

Harte: Yeah. I'm in Canada.

Marguerite: In Canada? Where exactly? Vancouver?

Harte: Inuvik.

Marguerite: Inuvik!

Harte: I had this ticket. I swear to God, we landed on an ice flow. Welcome to Canada. Unbelievable.

Marguerite: Good grief.

Harte: So I'm on my way. Bet you didn't believe I'd make it when I called from wherever I did. Where was that anyway?

Marguerite: Pakistan.

Harte: Pakistan. Well, I'm practically on your doorstep now.

Marguerite: Not on my doorstep, exactly. I wouldn't say that.

Harte: I'm in the right country at least.

Marguerite: How are you going to get here from Inuvik?

Harte: That's a problem. I'm kind of at the end of the line where my…prearranged travel is concerned. But I'll get there. Twin Otter to Yellowknife, I suppose. Then Yellowknife to Edmonton. Or Saskatoon. Christ, it's hot. You could roast a turkey.

Marguerite: It's hot? In Inuvik?

                Harte is seized by cramps. He can't talk.

              William? *(Pause.)* William, what's going on? Are you all right? *(Pause.)* Hello?

Harte: Just a little jet lag. I'll be fine after a good night's sleep.

Marguerite: I'd better give you directions.

Harte: What?

Marguerite: Directions to the house. How to find us.

Harte: Oh. Well, yeah, guess I need directions.

Marguerite: Have you got a pencil?

Harte: Yeah. Okay. Shoot.

Marguerite: All right. You can find your way to St. James, I presume. When you get there, go straight south on Highway 37. Have you got that?

Harte: *(Writing on his map.)* Yeah.

Marguerite: Six miles south of town you come to a set of railway
                tracks. Cross the tracks and turn west at the first grid.
                Then a kilometre in you'll come to three white grain
                bins. Turn south just past the bins and we're the first
                farm to the west. Did you get that?

Harte: First farm to the west. Yeah.

Marguerite: It's a blue house.

Harte: Blue house.

Marguerite: You can't miss it.

                Harte is seized by cramps again. He moans in pain.

                What's going on? What's the matter?

Harte: Marguerite, I gotta go. I'll get there as soon as I can.

Marguerite: Are you sure you're all right?

Harte: *(In serious pain.)* I'll be there in…say the day after
                tomorrow. If all goes well.

Marguerite: I'm looking forward to meeting you.

                *Harte hangs up and doubles over. Marguerite hangs
                up. Ruben rings his bell.*

Ruben: Marguerite?

                *Marguerite ignores him and finds Inuvik on her globe.
                Beauty and Harte fold up their maps.*

Scene 24

                *Joel is in bed with a pillow over his head. Marguerite
                is sitting on the edge of his bed.*

Marguerite: I know how you miss Stevie. I'm just trying to say that
                I understand that because…well sometimes, I miss
                having…company. Not that you and Ruben aren't
                good company. Definitely not. But I think
                kids…young people, teenagers…they get used to
                thinking of their parents as…well, mom or dad. You

know. Not people who…well, have needs that are very similar to the needs of people any age. Age doesn't matter, not where…companionship is concerned. It's not like I think about it all the time or anything, but once in a while, it occurs to me that… Well. Perhaps I've said enough. Do you know what I'm trying to say? *(No answer.)* Never mind. I don't suppose it will matter.

Marguerite leaves the room. Joel sits bolt upright.

Scene 25

       Lights on Harte.

Harte: St. James. That's it, that's what I'm looking for. That's the place. Phew. Hot. Son-of-a-bitchin' hot day. *(Pours water from his canteen over his head.)* Tired. So tired. My kingdom for a bed. Rest these bones.

Scene 26

       Marguerite has the table set with good china—four place settings. She's changed her hair.

       Ruben and Joel are in bed.

Marguerite: *(Calling.)* I want you up for dinner tonight. Both of you. I expect he'll be here for dinner. *(Pause.)* Are you planning to get up? Joel? Ruben?

Joel: I'm not feeling well. I'm sick.

Marguerite: And just what do you think you're sick with?

Joel: Whatever Ruben has.

Marguerite: You're such a smart-alec.

       Marguerite goes to Joel.

       Get up, Joel. You can't just lie in bed.

Joel: Why not?

Marguerite: What am I supposed to say when he gets here? "I'd introduce you to my son and my brother, but they're both in bed. For no particular reason, that I can see."

Joel: You don't have to say anything about us. We're none
               of his business.

Marguerite: He's a friend of your father.

Joel: Some friend.

Marguerite: What do you mean by that?

Joel: I know why you want Ruben and me to get up. Next
               you're going to tell us to get lost, leave you and Captain
               whoever-the-hell-he-is alone together.

Marguerite: You're going a little too far here, Joel. I've been lenient
               with you, but I have limits.

Joel: Maybe you do, but you can't make me get up.

               She goes to Ruben.

Marguerite: Get up, Ruben.

Ruben: I'm not hungry.

Marguerite: If you get up, maybe Joel will. *(Pause.)* Ruben. You
               have to get up. I'm not giving you a choice.

Ruben: I'm comfortable where I am, thanks anyway.

Marguerite: I insist.

Ruben: And I refuse.

Marguerite: It's my house.

Ruben: Are you the bloody queen now? I thought you were a
               little more democratic than that.

Marguerite: You have not been out of the house in a month. You've
               hardly been out of this room.

Ruben: I'm out of your hair, aren't I?

Marguerite: You can't live like this.

Ruben: *(Noticing her hair.)* What the hell have you done to
               yourself?

Marguerite: Don't change the subject.

Ruben: You've done something to your hair, haven't you?

Marguerite: Never mind what I've done...

Ruben: Jesus. You're like a schoolgirl, waiting for this...Captain somebody-or-other. Where's your dignity?

Marguerite: Forget about my dignity and think of your own for a change.

Ruben: It was you who put me in this bed, you know. Don't forget that.

Marguerite: And if you continue to expect me to wait on you hand and foot you're going to put me into an early grave.

Ruben: So, that's it. Let's worry about Marguerite now. That's the real truth of it, isn't it? Why don't you just call up the nursing home? Get rid of me once and for all.

Marguerite: You don't need a nursing home. You need to get up and walk around and breathe some fresh air once in a while.

Ruben: Don't give me that bullshit. You want to lock me up somewhere so I'll be out of your way. That's why you're always sticking this in my face... *(Grabs the cane and waves it around.)* So people can see me hobbling around and they'll say, "Look at Ruben. He should really be in a nursing home if he's that bad off."

Marguerite: Since when did you care what people say about you?

Ruben: Poor Marguerite. So much tragedy and now she's looking after that brother of hers.

Marguerite: You are an impossibly selfish man.

Ruben: You're never going to forget that I didn't want to stay here. That I wanted to do something else with my life.

Marguerite: I don't care about the past, Ruben. This is not about the past.

Ruben: You expect me to believe that? Anyway, you don't have me fooled. The nursing home's been your plan for me all along. Payback time. You've probably already talked to him about it.

Marguerite: Who?

Ruben: You know who. This Captain somebody-or-other. That's his real name, I imagine.

Marguerite: I'm not even sure I told him you're here. Now, I want you out of this bed. If you don't get out of bed, I will call the nursing home. I'll tell them to come and get you and good riddance.

Ruben: There we have it.

Marguerite: What?

Ruben: You said it. Call the nursing home.

Marguerite: You are impossible, you and Joel both. And I can't imagine what I've done to deserve either one of you.

Ruben: So, you think you deserve better. You admit that too. You're selfish, Marguerite.

Marguerite: I am not selfish.

Ruben: Always have been, always will be.

           Ruben is still waving the cane and he accidentally hits Marguerite.

           Marguerite. I didn't mean to...

Marguerite: I am not selfish.

           She leaves Ruben.

Ruben: Marguerite. I'm sorry, Marguerite.

Marguerite: Don't speak to me. Don't say another word.

           Marguerite picks up a plate and smashes it. Then she cleans it up.

Scene 27

           Harte is walking. It's early evening.

Harte: Sleep. Walking toward sleep. A feather bed. A bed of dust, dust and old bones, a bag of old bones in the dust. The dust billows and the bones rattle. A symphony, a lullaby. Sleep. *(Pause.)* Railway tracks. She said railway tracks.

He walks on.

Scene 28

> *The middle of the same night. Marguerite is asleep outside in one of the lawn chairs. Harte is in a lawn chair also, watching Marguerite. He looks terrible. Marguerite stirs, wakes up, sees Harte.*

Harte: Don't be scared. When I walked up and saw you sleeping...so peaceful. The chair was here and it just seemed...

Marguerite: Who are you?

Harte: *(Holding out his hand.)* We finally meet.

Marguerite: *(Not taking his hand.)* William?

Harte: I guess I should have stopped somewhere and cleaned up.

Marguerite: My God.

Harte: So. Here we are. You look...well, just exactly how I thought you'd look.

Marguerite: You're Captain Harte?

Harte: Captain Harte. That's me. Charlie started that, you know. He used to say, "Walk into any room, any situation and look around, you can pick out the man in charge. The one man in charge. That's you," he said to me. "That one man, the captain." Maybe once. Not now, hardly. Marguerite...

Marguerite: What?

Harte: Sorry to bother you, but do you think...could you get me a glass of water? I've been dreaming about water. Ice water.

Marguerite: Ice water.

Harte: I was in a hospital once and a nurse brought me ice water.

                He doubles over.

Marguerite: What's wrong?

Harte: Nothing much. Just a little fever.

Marguerite: *(Feeling his forehead.)* This is no little fever. You're burning up.

Harte: One thing's sure, I don't have syphilis. The high fever…it's an old cure. The nurse told me that. The one who brought me ice water. And the letter. It was the nurse who brought me your letter. And this picture… *(Struggles to get the picture.)*…this picture of you and Charlie and the two boys.

Marguerite: We have to get you to a hospital.

Harte: The boys…how are they?

Marguerite: The boys?

Harte: I don't remember their names.

Marguerite: You don't know… I thought that's why you called. Why you sent the flowers.

Harte: For Charlie. Flowers for Charlie.

Marguerite: I see. Well. Never mind. Can you stand?

Harte: I'll be all right. I'm here now, that's the main thing. Just need to rest these bones.

Marguerite: I'm taking you to town. Try to stand.

Harte: I'll be right as rain in the morning. Let me rest.

Marguerite: I won't hear of it. Try to stand now. That's it. Good.

                Harte tries to pick up his duffle bag.

                Here. Let me. This way. The car's this way.

                They move off.

Harte: Rattle of old bones.

Marguerite: What?

Harte: The rattle of old bones. Can you hear it?

Marguerite: I believe I can.

Scene 29

Hours later. Marguerite enters and sits in one of lawn chairs.

Marguerite: The sun's coming up. Another day. What could it possibly bring, except more of the same?

She sees the briefcase where Harte left it, picks it up and opens it. She looks through the contents and pulls out several tickets.

Cairo to Singapore. Gdansk to Istanbul. London to New Delhi. I wonder.

She puts the tickets back and closes the briefcase.

A waiter who blows in your ear. Not very likely, but worth a shot.

She exits, leaving the briefcase.

Scene 30

The audience sees all three men in bed. Harte is in a hospital bed. A nurse wearing latex gloves and a surgical mask fusses around him.

Harte: You're not Marguerite, are you?

Nurse: Shhhh. Just rest now, Mr. Harte.

Harte: Where is Marguerite?

Nurse: Mrs. Waker? She's gone home, I imagine. You're very lucky that she got you to a hospital. And you kicking up such a fuss about staying. You can't have a fever as high as yours and not do something about it. You just can't, Mr. Harte. Now go to sleep. We'll take good care of you.

The nurse exits.

Scene 31

> *Marguerite is trying to call Joel and Ruben from a pay
> phone. She has a small, practical bag for travelling
> light. The phone rings but no one answers it. Finally
> Joel stirs and lifts his head off the pillow.*

Joel: Is somebody going to get that? *(Pause.)* Mom, are you
               there? Get the phone. *(Pause.)* Somebody get the
               phone.

> *Joel puts the pillow over his head. The phone rings a
> few more times and then Marguerite hangs up.*

Scene 32

> *Harte's hospital room. The nurse enters.*

Nurse: How are we today?

Harte: Take a guess.

Nurse: Poor Mr. Harte. That fever is so hard on the body. But
               I think you're a little better. You're awake at least.

Harte: How long have I been here?

Nurse: Not too long. A week perhaps. Is there anything I can
               get you?

Harte: Ice water. I've been dreaming about ice water.

> *The nurse picks up a jug.*

Nurse: Of course. I'll pour it for you.

Harte: On me.

Nurse: Pardon?

Harte: Pour it on me.

Nurse: Pour it on you. I can't do that.

Harte: Call it a personal favour.

Nurse: I'll get you a cool cloth.

Harte: No cloth. Just the water. Settle the dust. Cool the
               bones.

Nurse:	Well. Perhaps just a bit.
	She dribbles some on his forehead.
	How does that feel?
Harte:	Like heaven. Has Marguerite been in?
Nurse:	Not yet.
Harte:	Don't stop. Ice water. Dust and old bones.
Nurse:	What's all this about bones?
Harte:	I keep hearing them.

Scene 33

Ruben is in bed. Joel has gotten out of bed and is sitting in a sea of empty pizza boxes. He's reading a postcard. He and Ruben call back and forth.

Joel:	I don't get it. "There is no Raoul." What the hell is that supposed to mean?
Ruben:	I'm a bit peckish.
Joel:	Not "Having a nice time" or "Wish you were here." Just, "There is no Raoul."
Ruben:	What time is it?
Joel:	I don't know.
Ruben:	My stomach's growling like an old engine.
Joel:	Yeah, well, maybe I'll go pick up a pizza.
Ruben:	Not with green peppers this time, I hope. I like green peppers, but they don't like me.
Joel:	Mushrooms. Olives.
Ruben:	Olives? I suppose I can pick them off. Pepperoni's good. We could try that.
Joel:	I suppose we ought to get a salad.
Ruben:	How about dessert, something different? I'm sick of ice cream. Cheesecake. How about cheesecake?

Joel:	You're being damned choosy for someone who won't lift a finger.
Ruben:	Well, I'm hungry.
Joel:	Just don't try ringing that bell. I'm more likely to shove it down your throat than bring you food on a tray.

Joel hears the sound of the Corvette. When it screeches to a stop, he goes outside to investigate.

What the hell was that?

Beauty enters, carrying her map. Something about her appearance throws Joel for a loop. An incredible head of dyed hair perhaps. Or tight leggings and high heels.

Beauty:	Hello?
Joel:	Uhh, hi.
Beauty:	I hope I have the right place.
Joel:	I don't know. What place are you looking for?
Beauty:	Marguerite Waker. I'm looking for Marguerite Waker's place.
Joel:	She's not here.
Beauty:	Oh.
Joel:	She lives here, but she's not here. Now. She's away.
Beauty:	Maybe you could help me.
Joel:	Me?
Beauty:	I'm looking for my husband.
Joel:	There's no husband here.
Beauty:	Oh.
Joel:	I was almost a husband once, but it didn't work out.
Beauty:	I'm sorry.
Joel:	That's okay. I'm almost over it. I guess. So you must have the wrong place.

Beauty:	There's no one here but you?
Joel:	Yeah. Well, me and my uncle.
Beauty:	Your uncle. What's his name?
Joel:	Ruben. Ruben McDonald. But he's not anybody's… He's not married. *(Gradually dawning on him who she is.)* I mean, he can't be…you couldn't be…
Beauty:	You know who I am?
Joel:	Ruben!
Beauty:	Wait. Do you think…will he want to see me?
Joel:	Why not? Ruben! You've got company.
Beauty:	I'm not sure he'll want to see me.
Joel:	Oh, yeah. He will.
Beauty:	Do you think so? `
Joel:	Trust me.
Beauty:	I can't imagine what you and your mother must think of me, his own wife.
Joel:	Huh?
Beauty:	I know it was cowardly, I can see that now.
Joel:	Well, never mind. We all…you know. We're not perfect, are we? Most of us.
Beauty:	You're very mature for a young man, Joel. That's right, isn't it? Your name is Joel?
Joel:	Yeah.
Beauty:	*(Holding out her hand.)* Pleased to meet you.
Joel:	Yeah. So you're my aunt, I guess.
Beauty:	I guess I am. But you don't have to call me "Aunt Beauty." Honestly, that name has been an albatross around my neck.
Joel:	Me and Ruben are kind of batching. You can probably tell.

Beauty: Looks like I arrived just in time.

Joel: I'd offer to make you something to eat but I don't know how to make anything. I'm a lousy cook. I was just going for pizza. You want some pizza?

Beauty: Forget pizza. It just so happens, Joel, that I am an excellent cook. Just show me to my husband and don't worry about a thing.

Joel: That way. Wow.

Beauty: Ruben?

Scene 34

Marguerite is in the Asian space, reading a tourist book.

Marguerite: *(Reading.)* "Travellers, almost without exception, have difficulty adjusting to the problems of heat and humidity. Although the high temperatures may seem unbearable, most people prefer summer with its dry heat to the monsoon season with its high humidity, floods and mosquito infestations. If there is one controlling force here, it is the weather, and travellers would be wise to accept that." *(Stops reading.)* Interesting. So universal.

She closes the book and exits.

Scene 35

Ruben and Joel are in lawn chairs. Ruben has the cane. Beauty brings them drinks with little umbrellas in them.

Beauty: Here you go. Cool drinks for a hot day.

Joel: Thanks.

Beauty: *(Dabbing sunscreen on them.)* Now, for a little bit of this. I'm sure I don't have to tell you about the hole in the ozone. Just a dab on your nose and the back of your neck.

Ruben: Can't say I care for the smell.

Beauty: Never mind. You have to put up with a few things in this life. That's just the way it is. Now don't sit out here for too long. It's not good for you. You really should be wearing hats, you know.

Joel: This is great. What's in it?

Beauty: A woman never gives away her secrets. Now, is there anything else I can get you boys?

Joel: No. I'm fine. Great.

Beauty: Ruben?

Ruben: I'm a bit peckish. But don't go to any trouble.

Beauty: Hummm. Something light, I think, for a hot day. A nice gazpacho.

Joel: Thanks.

            Beauty exits.

            Boy. She's something.

Ruben: What did I tell you?

Joel: Do you love her?

Ruben: Love her? Well, yeah.

Joel: I love Stevie.

Ruben: You could go there. To Vancouver.

Joel: Nah.

Ruben: Why not?

Joel: I think I'll hang around here for a while. Beauty's really something, eh?

Ruben: Yeah. And I think you should go to Vancouver.

Joel: Is she planning to stay?

Ruben: Did you see that ding she put in the right fender of my car? Ding? Size of a God damned coconut. Cars don't mean a thing to women, you know. Just something to get you from one place to another.

Joel: You're going to die, eh? From that disease.

Ruben: Hey. I'm not dead yet. A long way from it.

Scene 36

Marguerite is seated in the Asian space, waiting. She has a pen and postcard in her hand, thinking about what to write.

Marguerite: *(Thinking.)* Dear Joel. And Ruben. *(Writing.)* Dear Joel and Ruben. *(Thinking.)* I hope this finds you both… I hope I haven't… Rest assured that I'm… *(Writing.)* The weather here is definitely not what I'm used to. It's very hot and humid, although we're past the hottest season, and they say the humidity will rise in a month or so until it's close to the saturation point.

A nurse enters.

Nurse: Mrs. Waker?

Marguerite: Yes.

Nurse: The doctor will be a few more minutes. So many emergencies today.

Marguerite: There's no rush. I've just…it's nothing really. Just a little cut. But I was advised to get a prescription. The risk of infection…because of the climate.

Nurse: Absolutely true. Good advice. And I see you wisely brought something to do while you wait.

Marguerite: A card. To my family.

Nurse: Your children?

Marguerite: My son. I have…one son.

Nurse: A son. Very good. I have two children. Little ones. Life is never dull, is it, when you have children.

Marguerite: Never dull, no.

Nurse: They tire you out completely. Every night my children try to get into bed with my wife and me. Both of them. Even on the hottest nights.

Marguerite: I remember that, yes.

Nurse: Impossible to sleep, with their little bodies plastered to you. Maybe we were meant to be marsupials. A genetic mistake, this separation at birth. But never mind. They grow up, don't they? Your son is grown up?

Marguerite: Almost.

Nurse: Very good. Just a few more minutes. I'm sorry for the delay.

Marguerite: Thank you. *(Turning back to her card.)* The weather. *(Writing.)* You get used to it. You think you won't, but you do.

Scene 37

> *Mr. Sealey enters carrying a seedling, its roots in a burlap bag. He stops in Marguerite's garden. At the same time the audience sees Harte in his hospital bed.*

Mr. Sealey: Marguerite?

Harte: Marguerite?

> *Lights fade.*

> *The End.*

Printed in March 1999 by

ON DEMAND PRINTING INC.

in Longueuil, Quebec